Islamic Terrorism, ISIS, Iran, Iraq, Al-Qaeda, -
Are they Found in Bible Prophecy?

By J. Mike Byrd

January 2018

One might be asking, what is going on in this mad, mad world? Where is it all going? What is the solution to the ever-increasing worldwide threats of terrorism in the name of one of the world's largest religions? Does the Bible have any answers - is it relevant today? For almost 2000 years people have thought they were seeing current global developments fulfilling Bible prophecy - from Nero to Khrushchev and beyond. Is it just religious fanaticism, or reality-based predictions?   What is different now? If we let scripture speak for itself, which few have ever done, are there predictions that describe the threatening global developments of our time? Are there realistic answers? This book addresses these questions. The answers will surprise some, but may be essential to reality-based approaches to dealing personally, or collectively with an ever-degenerating global situation and developments.

Table of Contents

Introduction

What we will try to do in this book is deal with facts rather than speculation. As everyone likes to say - let's just stick with the facts. Of course the word "facts" in our relativistic society seems to be a matter of perception.   How about we start with just the facts that virtually everyone knows and accepts - not those debatable "facts" people argue about?

First, maybe we can start with widely recognized facts about what is going on in our world today. You may believe, as some do, that 911 was an inside job perpetrated by our own government (Bush did it) against ourselves. But probably no one is crazy enough to deny that militant Islam is spreading terror and committing horrendous acts of violence around our world today. Perhaps there are a few very uninformed pot-heads or computer/video gamers (or college students) who don't know about what is going on around the globe. They may not know who Al-Qaeda or ISIS is, or anything about the Islamic in-fighting in Syrian and Iraq, or about Iran's exportation of terror and quest for nuclear arms. But for those of us who are participating in the real world, these developments are realities we can't deny or ignore - even though many argue about the details, the causes and the solutions.

So, what is happening in our world? Who are the players on this world stage? What are the trends - where is it all headed? Many people do seem to be either somewhat oblivious to what is happening, or prefer to ignore it all, or are already tired of it all and prefer not to think too much about it. Those who are informed and do care probably feel helpless and somewhat pessimistic about the future of our world. Realistic answers that would inspire hope and confidence seem to be in short supply.

If we are to be optimistic about the future of our world - on what realities do we base this optimism? Is everything just going to work itself out? Will Islam just become the peaceful religion it is supposed to be (and has never been)? Do we just ignore it, submit to it, or try to fight it? Is there any real will to fight in the non-Islamic world? Can the western world - Europe and the US, survive economically or militarily without the mid-eastern oil controlled by Islamic governments? What do we do about Russia and China - will they become our allies in an overt struggle with an Islamic controlled bloc of nations such as prominent members of today's OPEC (Organization of Petroleum Exporting Countries)? Can Russia and China even survive economically without American and European markets and resources? Should we really bomb Iran, or let her have nuclear weapons? What happens when the Islamists get nuclear weapons? Or do they really even need more weapons of mass destruction when their propaganda and terror campaigns are so effective at neutralizing and paralyzing, if not defeating, their enemies? For example, what chance does Israel and the Jews, or for that matter Christians have in the court of world opinion? How do we stop Islamic terrorists at home or abroad without discriminating against a major religion, or profiling ethnic groups?

OK, ok, too many questions - any answers? Any credible solutions? Any realistic ideas or scenarios about how all of this is going to work out with a happy ending? World War I solved a global crisis, but set us up for Word War II. World War II left us with the cold war and the nuclear arms race - an era of peaceful coexistence by virtue of the threat of mutual destruction. The League of Nations, which was to usher in world peace, didn't work to well but gave us the United Nations. The United Nations has become an international breeding ground and clearinghouse for Political Correctness, to be manipulated and used by the very forces that have become the biggest threat to world peace. However it is a powerful force in the direction toward global unity via one-world government - just what the Fascists, Communists, and Islamists (to name but a few) all have always been committed to.

These were the solutions of global crises past - how well have they worked out for us? Indeed we have had decades of peace and prosperity in our part of the world - but now our prosperity is seen as irresponsible indulgence at the expense of the rest of the world (as in a zero-sum game - go figure). The threat of Communism has given way to the more imminent threat of Islamic expansionism - whose modest goal is world-wide dominance and control ("Islam" means "submission"). Can we realistically just hope that Islam will fall under its own weight as Communism did? If that is your hope - good luck! Dreamers and Utopians may feel better, but the feeling seems to fade away when reality sets in. Do we hope for another World War to eliminate or at least neutralize the threat? Perhaps, but who is up to the fight? Even conservative Republican Hawks in our beloved United States reject the notion of going to war - as in "troops on the ground" - to stop much of anything, much less the spread of the "peaceful religion." The few who suggest such a thing are marginalized by the media and the majority of political aspirants, who quite correctly point out that Americans have no stomach for another war, certainly not a nuclear war. And indeed - would anyone be the winner in the aftermath of such a war?

But even if someone had perfect answers, we live in such a pluralistic world that divisions between us (Socialism vs. Democracy, liberals vs. conservatives, left vs. right, Democrats vs. Republicans or Libertarians) seem to make it impossible for us to work together for any viable solution.

The "wise" men of our world, the intellectuals, and the enlightened masses who follow their lead, laugh at the "doomsday predictions" of those who take Bible prophecy seriously - and sometimes with good reason. But how intellectually enlightened is it to insist on the assumption that predictions, prognostications, or prophecies that warn of a very negative future involving a one-world government (the explicit goal of globalist so prominent in our world today) which becomes oppressive, are crazy and could never happen? **How far fetched is it to entertain the possibility that there could be an alliance between a major religious element and a powerful political and economic element, to become dominant on the world stage**? How laughable is a scenario perhaps involving a global government (one world government - admittedly the only solution to world wars) which would then destroy and suppress her enemies - oh say like the old Roman

Empire, or the Babylonian Empire, or the Islamic empire of the past - only on steroids? Can't happen, right? Lunatic fringe idea, right? Such are the enlightened opinions of men, who by the way, have no answers to all of the other questions raised - none that really make sense, or haven't been tried already with certifiable lack of success.

Proverbial wisdom tells us that the definition of insanity is to keep trying the same thing expecting a different outcome, or *"Those that fail to learn from history, are doomed to repeat it"* (Winston Churchill). Perhaps we could add to that another self-evident truth - **ignorance does not negate its own negative consequences**. Untested assumptions, perhaps based on what "everybody knows," is probably the most common and prevalent and dangerous form of ignorance. For most people in our world today it is almost common knowledge that Bible prophecy is at best nothing to be taken too seriously - just for the religious fanatics and the ignorant masses who want to believe in all that stuff. Apocalyptic or end-of-the-world-as-we-know-it messages and scenarios are the stuff of jokes and mockery of "bible-thumpers" and right-wing evangelical conservatives. Those who take the Bible seriously with respect to prophecy are characterized and portrayed as mostly religious nuts by the enlightened progressives of our day. And why not - **have any of their dire predictions ever come true**? Maybe that is a question to which one needs to determine the correct answer.

Down through time theories have come and gone especially about biblical predictions. Unfortunately some of the most well known theories, which are even popular today, may have discredited end-times Bible prophecy with respect to its credibility and reliability as a predictor of real-world developments and events. However, the widespread ignorance, and misgivings, and misinterpretations of Bible prophecy about the end-times won't make the realities go away. People who choose to ignore or reject the Bible as an authoritative source of information, especially in this realm of predictions, or prophecy, typically do so on the basis of untested assumptions. They normally make such choices about what to believe based on broad-based ignorance of the subject matter, perhaps emotion - but not for informed intellectual reasons.

The following sets forth some realities that can be ignored or denied, but not negated. First, we can begin with facts about what has happened historically, and what is happening now. Second, we can stick with facts about what the Bible does say, literally, taken in its natural sense. Ok, we may have to look at the preponderance of the evidence when it comes to the Bible, based on accepted scientific approaches and findings - such as the dating of the writing of some of the prophetic passages of scripture (the science being "Textual Criticism"). That means learning about and recognizing facts, or realities about Bible prophecy. It means answering the question, has the Bible proven to be accurate and reliable so far with respect to the many prophecies on the record for us to evaluate? Then it means examining carefully what it predicts for the future, and how well do those predictions seem to agree with what is happening in our world today? Only fools will ignore such easily verifiable realities, and that to their own peril.

There are enough virtually irrefutable facts to point us to some rational answers, which will be evident to all but the most biased and closed-minded skeptics (people who have other agendas than trying to get to facts, using criteria that is more emotional than logical and intellectual).

But then, **if God hasn't given us answers, who has or who will**? If His answers aren't in writing, as in a verifiably reliable source document, where will we go to find them? Do the events, developments and trends in our world match up to what is actually described in Bible prophecy? Has the Bible accurately predicted things that have happened already, with any credible degree of specificity? Are there objective reasons to believe that what is predicted in the Bible is about current developments, any more than any other time in the past? Even if the predictions are accurate and relevant to what is happening today, so what - does it matter, or is it helpful for us now, or will it be helpful in the future as things continue to progress?

It seems that for the majority in our world today the answers to these questions would be in the negative. That being the case, the answers to the questions posed in the preceding paragraphs don't seem to have any objective realistic answers or viable solutions. If God doesn't have answers for us, then who does? And if we don't like the answers we find in God's revelations to us, what then? Do we reject them, or ignore them, and look for answers more to our liking? Perhaps for most this is the real question that would even cause them to prefer to remain as ignorant as possible on this whole subject - after all, their personal reality is as good as anyone else's, right? Maybe not so much!

    Well that is what this book is about. What are the realities in our world today? What does the Bible really have to say about them? What is the track record with respect to the accuracy of biblical predictions, or prophecies? If Bible prophecy is predictive of coming realities, what can we expect and what should we do about it, if anything? We report, you decide.

Chapter 1 What in the World is Going On?

What is Happening?

Here is a fairly random sampling, a snapshot of news stories over the last few years.

- **ISIS: The first terror group to build an Islamic state?**
(By Tim Lister, CNN Updated 11:25 PM ET, Thu June 12, 2014)
"The face of a balding, middle-aged man stares unsmilingly into the camera. He is dressed in a suit and tie and could pass for a midlevel bureaucrat. But the photograph is that of Abu Bakr al Baghdadi, who has transformed a few terror cells harried to the verge of extinction into the most dangerous militant group in the world. The Islamic State in Iraq and Syria has thrived and mutated during the ongoing civil war in Syria and in the security vacuum that followed the departure of the last American forces from Iraq. The aim of ISIS is to create an Islamic state across Sunni areas of Iraq and in Syria. With the seizure of Mosul, Iraq's second-largest city, and advances on others, that aim appears within reach.
ISIS controls hundreds of square miles where state authority has evaporated. It ignores international borders and has a presence all the way from Syria's Mediterranean coast to south of Baghdad."
(http://www.cnn.com/2014/06/12/world/meast/who-is-the-isis/index.htm)

- **Beheadings, torture by ISIS terrorize Iraq**
(CNBC - video, Tuesday, 12 Aug 2014 | 7:00 PM ET)
"NBC's Keir Simmons reports on the violent acts committed by the Islamic State and how Iraqis are running from the group's terror." (https://www.cnbc.com/video/2014/08/12/beheadings-torture-by-isis-terrorize-iraq-.html)

- **US admits there is a much scarier terrorist group than ISIS (**Published time: September 21, 2014 12:23 Edited time: September 23, 2014 09:37)
"New intelligence has emerged warning Washington that its upcoming confrontation with the Islamic State may leave it blind to a more sinister and direct threat from a much lesser

known terrorist group that has arisen from the ashes of the Syrian war.

Very little information is being released at the moment by anyone within American intelligence circles, but the group calling itself Khorasan is said by officials to have concrete plans for striking targets in the United States and Europe as a chosen modus operandi – more so than the Islamic State (IS), formerly known as ISIS."

(http://rt.com/usa/189448-khorasan-terrorist-qaeda-isis-syria/)

- **ISIS kills 400, mostly women & children, in Palmyra – Syrian state TV** (Published time: 24 May, 2015 11:08)

 "Islamic State fighters have killed at least 400 people, including women and children, in Palmyra since capturing the ancient Syrian city four days ago, Syrian state media said on Sunday, citing residents. (https://www.rt.com/news/261621-syria-palmyra-isis-civilians/)

- **Boston Terror Suspect: Beheading By ISIS Targeted...** (INQUISITR, Jun 03, 2015)

 "ISIS terror suspect Usaamah Rahim had planned to target Pamela Geller for beheading, but grew weary of waiting for his jihad moment and chose to take aim at the "boys in blue," according to reports. Two hour prior to the Boston police confrontation, terror suspect Rahim was already beginning to abandon his beheading target, Pamela Geller, and reportedly said he was going after Boston police because they were an "easy target." …(www.inquisitr.com/2143510/boston-terror-suspect)

- **The Iranian Nuclear Threat: Why it Matters -** (ADL EXTREMISM, TERRORISM & BIGOTRY)

WHY IS IRAN'S NUCLEAR WEAPONS PROGRAM A THREAT TO AMERICA AND AMERICAN INTERESTS?

"Nuclear weapons in the hands of the Iranian regime will have severe repercussions for American security and the security of our allies.

   o A nuclear-armed Iran would embolden Iran's aggressive foreign policy, resulting in greater confrontations with the international community. Iran already has a conventional weapons capability to hit U.S. and allied troops stationed in the Middle East and parts of Europe. If Tehran were allowed to develop nuclear weapons, this threat would increase dramatically.

o Iran is one of the world's leading state sponsors of terrorism through its financial and operational support for groups such as Hezbollah, Hamas, and others. Iran could potentially share its nuclear technology and know-how with extremist groups hostile to the United States and the West.

o While Iranian missiles can't yet reach America, Iran having a nuclear weapons capability can potentially directly threaten the United States and its inhabitants. The U.S. Department of Defense reported in April 2012: 'With sufficient foreign assistance, Iran may be technically capable of flight-testing an intercontinental ballistic missile by 2015.' Many analysts are also concerned about the possibility of a nuclear weapon arriving in a cargo container at a major US port. Furthermore, a federally mandated commission to study electromagnetic pulse (EMP) attacks noted the vast damage that could be wrought by a single missile with a nuclear warhead, launched from a ship off the US coast, and detonated a couple of hundred miles in the air, high above America.

o A nuclear-armed Iran poses a threat to America's closest allies in the Middle East. Israel is most at risk as Iran's leaders have repeatedly declared that Israel should 'be wiped from the map.' America's moderate Arab allies, such as Saudi Arabia, UAE, Bahrain, and others are already alarmed at Iran's aggressive regional policy and would feel increasingly threatened by a nuclear-armed Iran.

o The Middle East remains an essential source of energy for the United States and the world. Iran's military posture has led to increases in arms purchases by its neighbors. A nuclear-armed Iran would likely spark a nuclear arms race in the Middle East that would further destabilize this volatile and vital region.

HOW DO WE KNOW IRAN IS DEVELOPING NUCLEAR WEAPONS? Iran's nuclear program is clearly intended to develop a nuclear weapons capability. For eighteen years, it was kept secret, even though international assistance would have been available to a civilian program. In 2002, Iran's covert program was exposed. Since then, the International Atomic Energy Agency (IAEA) has repeatedly said that it cannot consider Iran's nuclear program as entirely civilian. On November 8, 2011 it released a report stating there is 'credible' evidence that 'Iran has carried out activities relevant to the development of a nuclear device.' Each report since then has underscored Iran's continuing refusal to address the IAEA's evidence and its refusal to allow IAEA inspectors into the Parchin complex, where evidence shows 'strong indicators of possible nuclear weapon development.'

In 2009, Western intelligence agencies discovered, and Iran admitted to, another secret facility that is designed for approximately 3,000 centrifuges to enrich uranium. President Obama commented that the 'configuration' of the Fordow facility is 'not consistent with a peaceful nuclear program.' Three thousand centrifuges are sufficient for producing quantities of highly enriched uranium for nuclear weapons, but not for fuel for nuclear power plants."

- **Iran and Terrorism - State Sponsored Terrorism in Iran - "Iran, State Sponsor of Terrorism"** (ThoughtCo., By Amy Zalman, Ph.D., Updated May 25, 2017):

"Iran has consistently been described by the United States as the world's foremost state sponsor of terrorism. It actively supports terrorist groups, most prominently the Lebanese group Hezbollah. The Iranian relationship with Hezbollah demonstrates one accepted explanation of why states sponsor terrorism: to indirectly influence politics elsewhere."
(https://www.thoughtco.com/state-sponsored-terrorism-in-iran-3209201)

- **Religion and Conflict in Syria "Is the Conflict in Syria a Religious War?"** (ThoughtCo., By Primoz Manfreda, updated August 18, 2017)

"Religion plays an important role in the conflict in Syria.
A United Nations report in late 2012 said that the conflict was becoming "overtly sectarian" in some parts of the country, with Syria's various religious communities finding themselves on the opposite sides of the fight between the government of President Bashar al-Assad and Syria's fractured opposition.

Growing Religious Divide

At its core, the civil war in Syria is not a religious conflict. The dividing line is one's loyalty to the Assad's government. However, some religious communities tend to be more supportive of the regime than the others, fuelling mutual suspicion and religious intolerance in many parts of the country. Syria is an Arab country with a Kurdish and Armenian minority. In term of religious identity, most of the Arab majority belongs to the Sunni branch of Islam, with several Muslim minority groups associated with the Shiite Islam. The Christians from different denominations represent at least 10% of the population.

The emergence among the anti-government rebels of hard-line Sunni Islamist militias fighting for an Islamic state has alienated the minorities. The outside interference from the Shiite Iran and the Sunni Saudi Arabia makes matter worse, feeding into the wider Sunni-Shiite tension in the Middle East."
(https://www.thoughtco.com/religion-and-conflict-in-syria-2353551)

- **Saudi FM: Iran 'number one state sponsor of terrorism'**
(Aljazeera News/Saudi Arabia10 Nov 2017)

"Adel al-Jubeir said 'Iran is the number one state sponsor of terrorism' in an interview with US television network CNBC that aired on Thursday. (http://www.aljazeera.com/news/2017/11/saudi-fm-seeks-pressure-iran-hezbollah-171109193012811.html")

- **What Did Isis Do In 2017? Islamic State Reveals Its Favorite Terror Attacks And Calls For More**
(Eye on Extremism: Newsweek: November 20, 2017)

"The Islamic State militant group revealed Thursday a list of what it considered to be its most prominent attacks around the world this year and called for more deadly violence. ISIS, by most accounts, was effectively defeated as a war fighting force in 2017, but its ability to strike without warning in major cities across the globe remains a serious security issue for countries contributing to the multinational battle against the jihadis, mostly in Iraq and Syria. Capitalizing on its residual influence on social media, ISIS included in the latest issue of its weekly digital magazine Al-Naba an evaluation of its attacks abroad throughout the Islamic calendar year of 1438, which lasted from

October 3, 2016, to September 21, 2017. Noting that 'figures include only officially endorsed operations,' the group counted 38 operations conducted by 60 jihadis in 19 countries this year. The list of nations included Australia, Bangladesh, Belgium, Egypt, France, Germany, Indonesia, Iran, Italy, Jordan, Kenya, Palestine, Russia, Spain, Sweden, Tunisia, Turkey, the U.K. and the U.S." (https://www.counterextremism.com/roundup/eye-extremism-november-20-1)

• **Egypt Massacre In Sinai May Point To An Even More Bloody IS** (Eye on Extremism: Washington Post, December 4, 2017) "The massacre of more than 300 worshippers at a mosque in Egypt's Sinai crossed a new line — even by militants' brutal standards — and could be a sign the Islamic State group is trying to make up for the loss of its 'caliphate' in Iraq and Syria or that an even more ultra-extremist faction is rising in power. Either way, if the IS affiliate in Sinai does have a new readiness to slaughter Muslims, that threatens to put a further strain on Egypt's security forces and intimidate anyone cooperating with the government in the fight against militants. But it also could raise a backlash against IS, prompting Sinai tribes to cooperate with the military and take greater action to stop any of their members from joining the group."
(https://www.counterextremism.com/roundup/eye-extremism-december-4-1)

• **Islamic State Claims Deadly Blast at Afghan Shiite Center** (The New York Times, by Fahim Abed Fatima Faizi, and Mujib Mashal, Dec. 28, 20017)
"At least 41 people were killed and dozens more wounded on Thursday in a bombing at a Shiite cultural center in Kabul that also houses a news agency, Afghan officials said. The Islamic State has claimed responsibility for the attack. It was the latest in a series of mass-casualty attacks against Shiite targets by the militant group's Afghan affiliate. The United Nations mission in Afghanistan has documented more than a dozen attacks since January 2016, with hundreds of Shiites dead or wounded. One of the deadliest was in October, when suicide bombers killed at least 57 worshipers in a Shiite mosque in Kabul, the capital, and injured dozens more. 'I have little doubt that this attack deliberately targeted civilians,' said Toby Lanzer, the acting

head of the United Nations mission in Afghanistan. 'Today in Kabul we have witnessed another truly despicable crime in a year already marked by unspeakable atrocities.'"
(https://www.nytimes.com/2017/12/28/world/asia/afghanistan-suicide-attack.html)

- **Terror Attacks Are Likely To Increase In 2018, With ISIS And Al-Qaeda Both Still Dangerous** (CNBC, by Natasha Turak, 9:32 PM ET Thu, 28 Dec 2017)

"The 'caliphate' may be in ruins, but that doesn't mean ISIS is gone forever. Terror attacks are likely to increase in 2018, as the destruction of the Islamic State's physical stronghold in Iraq and Syria will strengthen its will to strike out abroad, experts say. 'ISIS will want to show that they are still in the fight, and their followers remain as fanatical as ever,' said Lewis-Sage Passant, a former British Army intelligence officer and founder of travel security company How Safe Is My Trip. 'The number of attacks globally will likely increase as the group switches focus from the war in the Middle East to international terrorism.'"
(https://www.cnbc.com/2017/12/28/terror-isis-and-al-qaeda-likely-to-carry-out-more-attacks-in-2018.html)

- **The US Military Is Fighting Terrorism In 76 Countries Around The World — Here's Where** (Eye on Extremism: Business Insider, *January 15, 2018*)

"'This crusade, this war on terrorism is going to take a while,' former President George W. Bush said on the White House South Lawn on Sept. 16, 2001. 'And the American people must be patient. I'm going to be patient.' Bush was right that a war on an abstract noun like 'terror' would take awhile. It began in October 2001 with the US' invasion of Afghanistan. And although former President Barack Obama officially ended 'The Global War on Terror' in 2013, the fight against terrorism continues nearly 17 years later. In fact, it has spread. Between October 2015 and October 2017, the US fought terror in 76 countries, or 39% of the total number of countries in the world, according to data recently published by Brown University's Costs of War Project. (https://www.counterextremism.com/)

Well we do have one explanation for what is going on as posted on the Muslim-academy.com website:

"Spread of Islam in Europe" (Muslim-academy.com November 2012)
"Islam religion is gaining popularity in the whole world because it is true religion. In 1970, there was no mosque present in France, but now more than 3000 mosques are present. It shows the rapid spread of Islam teachings in European countries. Tableghi jammats are playing a great role in the spread of Islam in Europe. Now the members of this jammats are present in the whole world. Similarly, Islamic scholars are doing their work in a better way. Now Islam has become fastest growing religion in the whole world. Hundreds of people enter into Islam daily. **Islam is a peaceful religion and it focuses on equal rights for women**. Similarly Islam focuses on rights of neighbors and relatives. **People of other religions feel this religion is best of all**. Therefore followers of Islam are increasing in the world with the passage of time. It is a real fact that soon this religion will become the largest religion in the world" (emphasis added). (http://muslim-academy.com/spread-of-islam-in-europe/).

On the one hand we have the facts reported in the news. On the other we have the explanations and claims of the adherents and proponents of the same ideology and religion that is constantly making the news. What should we believe - actions, or words?

This is the world we live in. This is what is going on today in this mad mad world.

So What?

Now every informed, educated politically-correct member of the mainstream of society in our enlightened age knows that Islam is a peaceful religion - right? But like the stupid little boy asking why the emperor doesn't have any clothes on, one might be tempted to ask why do we have so many violent, militaristic organizations, including many indisputably recognized terrorist organizations operating around the world - all in the name of this "peaceful religion"? The following is a partial list of such organizations provided by Patrick Sookhdeo (in his book <u>Global Jihad - The Future in the Face of Militant Islam</u>):

- Shia Muslim:
    1. Hizb al-Dar'wa al-Islamiyya (Islamic Da'wa Party - mostly in Iraq)
    2. Hizbullah (mostly in Iran and Lebanon)
- Sunni Muslim - Arabic
    1. Hamas
    2. Hizb ut-Tahrir
    3. Qubist Jihadi: Tanzim al-jihad, al-Jama's al-Islamiyya
    4. Qubist Tadfiri: Takfir wal Hijra, Salsfist Group for Call and Combat (GSPC)
    5. Salafi-Wahha i-al-tawhid wal Jihad
    6. Laskar Juhad (Indonesia)
- Sunni - Indian sub-continent
    1. Deobandi - Harakat-ul Mujahideen (HUM), Harakat-ul-Jihad-Al-Islami (HUJI), Taliban, Jaish-e-Mohammed (JEM), Sipah-i-Sahaba
    2. Jamat'at-i-Illmai - Hizb-ul Mujahideen (HM)
    3. Ahl-i-Hadith - Lashkar-e-Tayyiba
- Sunni - global
    1. Salafi-Jihadi - al Qa'eda, Jema'ah Islamiyah
    2. Muslim Brotherhood
    3. Hizb ut-Tahrir

Today (2018) we hear everyday in the news about ISIS (Islamic State of Iraq and Syria) or simply IS (Islamic State) or ISIL (Islamic State of Iraq and Levant). In Nigeria we have Boko Haram. The horrific reports and videos that are almost daily international news, shock most of us and are met with revulsion, as we marvel at how people can be so inhumane and evil? And one of the latest (as of this writing) is Khorasan, which makes its threats directly against the United States and Europe. What would happen if we had a religion which wasn't peaceful, if this is what we get from one that is peaceful? Or the honest question is, how could anyone be so audacious as to tell such grandiose lies - for that matter, how could anyone believe such total fabrications which contradict all of the available evidence not only from history, but that is in our face on the news everyday? Are normal human beings, on such a large scale, really capable of such incomprehensible evil, and such incredible lies, and being so inexplicably deceived - without some element of the supernatural? How does a religion with such a bloody history (beginning with its founder Mohammed), and such a widely known reputation for violence and bloodshed, become accepted by intelligent people (indeed, intellectuals) as a "peaceful religion"?

Ok, the argument is that not all Muslims are violent, or militant, or terrorist. That is certainly true, and no one should paint them all with a broad brush any more than all Christians should be judged by the actions of the Crusaders, or the abuses of the Catholic church, or a few aberrant activists who have bombed abortion clinics, or protest at funerals of our military heroes.   However, the easily verifiable fact is that this religion's holy book, the Koran (Quran), gives the so-called radical extremists the scriptural authority for their violent and extremists' militarism. The Prophet Mohammed himself set the example, which they now follow - this is simply a matter of the historic record. It is also true that the Koran is full of contradictions - so its defenders can point to some passages that teach peace and tolerance. But to characterize the whole book as advocating tolerance and peaceful coexistence with infidels, and Christians and Jews, is to blatantly distort and deny the truth. Furthermore we have the Hadiths, and the writings and teaching of many highly respected Islamic clerics and Imams and even Caliphs, which have been and are being obeyed by those radical extremists down to the present time. Anyone who has bothered to inform themselves about Islamic eschatology knows very well that the universally accepted mission and goal of Islam is to completely dominate if not eradicate all infidels, Jews, and non-Muslims - hence the name "Islam."

Denial - whether its about addiction, or cancer, or any kind of threat to one's perceived well-being - is deadly. Yet without it, most threats could be dealt with and overcome in healthy ways. In recent history we have the now infamous record of how people in power, most famously Prime Minister Chamberlain of Great Britain, chose to deny the threat of Adolph Hitler and Nazism, despite all the evidence available to them. We all know the outcome, but their denial is nothing compared to what is being almost universally accepted by leaders of the "free-world" today. Where is all of this heading? Is the threat not that real - not that big of a deal? Is the openly declared enemy not really an enemy - no matter what they do and say? This is Chamberlainism on steroids! There seems to be a "strong delusion" that defies explanation in natural human terms - can intelligent people, or even just average people, be so blind and stupid?

It appears as though Sir Winston Churchill may be right again, just as he was about Hitler when he said, *"Those that fail to learn from history, are doomed to repeat it."* It looks like we are in the process of repeating it, only this time the consequences for the world will likely be far worse - unless and until some Messiah figure shows up on the scene who can do something about it.

It is also becoming quite apparent that such a Messiah figure, maybe even a 21st century Ronald Reagan, or a Margaret Thatcher, isn't going to come from Europe, nor from the Democrat party or even the Republican party of the United States. Probably not even President Trump despite his best efforts, will likely prevent the inevitable, though like President Reagan, he may be able to delay it. The cows are out of the barn, the cancer has progressed to a stage that has no remedy - it is fatal. What western leader, or non-Islamic leader will now be able to reign in the rapidly spreading disease that is radical Islam? When we capture or kill a Bin-Laden the snake metastasizes into a dozen more which are more deadly than he ever was. Who will be able to either corral or negotiate with that kind of enemy - short of nuclear war, which would lead to a holocaust in which there would be no winners, if any survivors.

Maybe some progressive, optimistic wizards of smart can come up with an idea or plan which hasn't already been tried unsuccessfully - I for one can't even imagine what that would be, realistically speaking.

Now who is looking like the crazy fools of our time (as in out-of-touch-with-reality)? Is it those who can entertain the notion that we may be looking at a rather gloomy future for the world? Are the idiots those who can see a much sought after "one-world-government," but not the utopia liberals and progressives are hoping for? Are out-of-touch fools those who are able to realistically assess the global situation and trends, and can see a universal global Caliphate as a very real possibility? Or would it more likely be those who choose denial, and just want to believe that this too shall pass somehow - those who can't even consider an end-of-the-world scenario, as seen by some "religious fanatics" who take Bible prophecy seriously?

Of course by the time this book is read by anyone the news stories cited above will be old news - history. They will be replaced by news of newer developments - some of which could give rise temporarily to optimism and hope. These dire trends we have been seeing at the time of this writing could change, as we saw occurred with the election of conservatives in the Reagan era. There is a great deal of optimism and hopeful trends both nationally and even globally since the election of another conservative president and congress. We even already see a backlash in some of the Islamic community to all of the extreme violence of groups such as ISIS. We see some of the Islamic countries (such as Saudi Arabia, Jordan, possibly Egypt) beginning to work together to resist not only ISIS, but Iran, as they are very threatened by her overt expansionism. The United States appears to be taking the lead in doing something about the global Islamic threat. Furthermore, we see mostly in-fighting between Islamists, especially Sunni against Shia, which could make one hope that they will self-destruct. Such reversals and encouraging trends will make all this dooms-day talk again become material for stand-up comics to make fun of the religious Bible prophecy nuts.

A very possible, and perhaps not unlikely scenario is that these radical extremists, who we are told have just "hijacked the religion," will actually be opposed and possibly even neutralized by a coalition of more moderate Muslims. It is not inconceivable that **a strong leader will emerge in the Islamic world, who will oppose and defeat the more violent extremists**. Such a leader may be able to gain the support of enough of the Islamic masses, which are the more peaceful Muslims (which we are being told is the majority of all Muslims) to come to power. But perhaps just as importantly **such a leader will be enthusiastically embraced by the rest of the world, the non-Islamic world, the western world in particular, as a heroic savior for the whole world**. Since the world has been led to believe that Islam is really a peaceful religion, the fact that he will be a Muslim, from a Muslim country, will not even be an issue - if he can put an end to the global terrorism. He will in fact be **the Messiah figure almost everybody is looking for** - except for the true Christians and Jews. Just as Nobel Peace Prize winner Anwar Sadat was hailed as a great peacemaker because he accepted a deal with Israel's Prime Minister Begin, bringing a short-lived peace between Egypt and Israel, so a modern version of Sadat could win the confidence of the western world (U.S. and Europe) by agreeing to a peace treaty with Israel.

Then, if this moderate Islamist becomes the dominant leader of the Islamic world, he would also be in control of the world's most essential resource - oil. With the oil comes almost unlimited wealth, but even more importantly, power. OPEC (Organization of the Petroleum Exporting Countries), and in particular Saudi Arabia, has proven it has the power to virtually control the global oil markets. Those OPEC nations are all Islamic except for two, Ecuador and Venezuela (who are no match for Saudi Arabia and Iran). While Russia may have her own supply of oil, her economy can be devastated by manipulations of supply, and hence the price of oil on the world markets. Similarly, economies around the world, including United States and Canada and Mexico, are very much affected by such manipulations, as we saw in the 1974 oil crises, and again in the 2012 slashing of the price of oil. Much has changed since, yet much remains the same. If they (OPEC and in particular Saudi Arabia) decrease the supply (by reducing either production or exportation) they can cause price increases that hurt the economies of the rest of the world, probably by inflation, and forcing reduced consumption. If they increase the supply they can bring the price of oil down, such that competitors such as the United States will be driven out of much of the market - as in the last few years as oil wells were shut down and shale oil and fracking (hydrofracturing) production became less profitable. Such manipulations also have dramatic effects on stock markets, which are now international.

Europe is of course extremely vulnerable and dependent upon OPEC oil. While the U.S. has recently been able to produce more than half of its own demand, that has been largely because of the high price of oil. That has since changed mostly because of major oil producing countries like Saudi Arabia's attempt to eliminate those more expensive methods of oil production as competitors on the world markets. However, the United States without her European allies and trade partners would be in a very vulnerable position, even if she were mostly independent from OPEC oil (consider the high anxiety at home as well as abroad over the precarious status of the European Common Market, over the threat of bankruptcy and default by Greece). Just the threat of such a development may well be enough to paralyze her (the U.S.) with respect to taking any affective action against such a powerful bloc of nations - certainly not military action against them (i.e. troops on the ground).

China was recently leading the U.S. as the world's largest importer of foreign oil, most of which is probably middle-eastern oil. Russia is a major exporter of oil, but her economy suffers when the price of oil drops. Both Russia and China, like the U.S., depend upon western markets to thrive economically. They know that if the western economies fall it will bring them down as well. But they will also know they cannot afford to alienate the Islamic oil producers who will have the power to manipulate the petroleum markets, and bring down the economies which global commerce - their own lifeline - depends upon. The reality is that we now live in a global community with respect to markets and commerce, and even the stock markets.

However, the modern industrialized economies are much more vulnerable than the slightly more primitive cultures found in many of those Islamic oil producing countries whose consumption of not only natural resources but manufactured goods is far less - and when it comes to oil they are rich. Their wealth also means that they can always buy anything else they need from someone greedy or desperate enough to sell their products (witness the U.S. secretary of state in the Obama/Clinton era being bought off by Swedish business executives to allow them exemptions from the economic sanctions being used to force Iran to stop their nuclear arms development).

Furthermore elected leaders of the western "free world" democracies know they have to protect and preserve their high standards of living with high rates of consumption, in order to stay in power ("it's the economy stupid"). On the other hand, that is not the highest priority in those countries which are perhaps not as democratic as they profess to be, but tend to be centralized governments characterized more by centralized planning than representative governance (as in Iran, or Syria, or Turkey - most if not all of the Islamic nations).

If then there is to be a coalition of those Islamic oil producing nations under one leader, without the current competition between them, such manipulations of oil production and export could be a very lethal weapon in that coalition's war against her enemies. Even without weapons of mass destruction (WMD) the rest of the world could be brought to its knees economically by the strategic manipulation of the one resource of which they have an abundance. But, then if they do have WMD, and in particular nuclear weapons, the rest of the world will be intimidated into paralysis knowing that they will very likely use those WMD and nuclear weapons - which no one else is willing to do (until it is too late), and for good reasons.

Perhaps the only rational thing to do is to assess the situation realistically (rather than just optimistically or hopefully), and to consider the possibility that we may actually be looking at a doomsday, end of the world as we know it, scenario. Ironically, world leaders are crying "the sky is falling," with doomsday end of the world scenarios about an imagined threat of "global warming," which they now have to rename as "climate change" (since there isn't really any warming since 1997). While blatantly lying about the consensus of scientists,* and "settled science," they buy into a theory that has actually no scientific basis in fact (actual measurements of atmospheric temperatures show a slight decline in average global temperature over the last 18 years - the contribution of man-made CO2 to the atmospheric gases is less than 0.0013 % or 13 parts per million - do the math). Rather it is a classic case of the political perversion of science, which conveniently for them circumvents the scientific method, and plays on the ignorance and gullibility of the masses, and the useful idiots in the media. One thing is sure, if such a threat is real it will be the end of the world because there is nothing those who believe in it can do about it, especially when the major polluting nations around the world (such as China and India) don't buy into it - probably in part because they know it is a hoax. The point is that while the wizards of smart are mocking those who see the real and undeniable very present threat as having doomsday potential, they gullibly and unquestionably embrace a far-fetched unrealistic threat as being more threatening, demanding our immediate attention and major sacrifices on our part. Go figure.

*[One of many examples, the Petition Project, is a survey of more than **31,000** physicists and physical chemists (more than 9,000 with a Ph.D. - by far the most signatures) which agree with the statement that "there is no convincing scientific evidence that human release of . . . carbon dioxide, methane, or other greenhouse gases is causing or will, in the foreseeable future, cause catastrophic heating of the Earth's atmosphere and disruption of the Earth's climate."]

Again, what in the world is going on here? How do we explain this madness? Islam is not a threat, but "climate change" deniers are a real threat we need to do something about - as are evangelical Christians and religious Jews, and for that matter right wing conservatives - really?

I have no delusions of grandeur that most or even many people will have their minds changed by anything discussed above - real facts and logic don't matter much to either the most enlightened progressive thinkers of our time, or the relatively ignorant and easily manipulated masses (and never has). But for the few sober minded discriminating logical thinkers who are more interested in reality and getting to the naked truth at the heart of the matter, maybe it will be food for serious thought. Maybe they will realize that it might be wise to take another look at the Bible and what it has to say about the past, present and future. Maybe one should start at looking at what has been predicted in the Bible, and see if those predictions proved to be accurate.* Then one might look at what is predicted about the so-called "end-times," and see if it aligns with what we see going on in our world today. We might objectively and critically evaluate the answers to those questions raised above as given in the Bible, and even compare it to the answers contemporary "wise men" of our age are giving us.   Then we have to rationally choose which is more believable and realistic.

*[Interestingly enough the widely proclaimed imminent threat of "climate change" with claims of tenths of a degree Celsius increase in global temperature, are based on unproven climate models, none of which have been validated (as they should be to be taken seriously) by having made accurate predictions given past data inputs. The Bible on the other hand, has made many predictions with respect to global developments - a validation that modern computer models lack entirely. Which is scientific? Which should be taken seriously?]

The next chapter delves into the track record with respect to Biblical predictions, or prophecy - for many it may come as a big surprise, if they can open their minds to look objectively at the real evidence (which probably won't be that many - just being a realist here).

Chapter 2   Has the Bible ever gotten it right?

"...people are destroyed for lack of ***knowledge"*** *(Hosea 4:6)*
"...my people are gone into captivity, because they have
no knowledge" *(Isaiah 5:13)*

What Do We Really Know?

We live in an age, a self-proclaimed "enlightened age," when it is acceptable, normal, even fashionable or smart, to speak out authoritatively about things we know little or next to nothing about. That is very much related to believing things that we haven't really checked out, usually because we already know what is right - we think. Unfortunately what we are so cock sure is right, tends to be what we want to believe is right, or what we think some mainstream majority believes is right (i.e. groupthink). This is of course nothing new to our age. In fact we laugh about what people before us believed and were so cock sure was true - the world was definitely flat, and the sun, moon, planets and stars obviously revolved around the earth. The nuts who didn't believe such mainstream facts were "outliers," maybe some kind of religious nuts, or just plain stupid. Ok who were the stupid ones now?

But we have arrived now - we are more enlightened. What is common knowledge now, mainstream beliefs, because now we know sooo much, is all true - we have evolved to the point we don't need to question what the experts tell us now (that is the experts we prefer to listen to). Whereas such knowledge and beliefs are changing every day, making yesterday's knowledge and beliefs outdated and looking kind of foolish, we can be completely confident what we believe today, this very hour, is it - finally the right answers, the ultimate truth. Really? How naïve!

Hopefully the reader is intelligent enough, and rational enough, to see something wrong with this kind of thinking, and these kinds of attitudes. Yesterday, a few years ago, we knew what everything was made of - tiny tiny particles called atoms.

Oops, but then we discovered those atoms were actually a little tiny solar system of particles, called protons and neutrons at the center (nucleus), and electrons orbiting around them (and now its leptons (with electrons, muons and neutrinos) and baryons (with neutrons and protons) and photons, quarks, gluons, mesons and bosons, and for all the particles we have antiparticles, and some of these particles have many different states, and on and on). Now we have it figured out - we know what all matter is.

But wait, it seems that these microscopically small (requiring electron microscopes) particles aren't really just particles at all - they act more like waves in certain experiments - though even Einstein was sure at one time they had to be particles of matter, which he later changed his mind about. But they couldn't be both at the same time, as Einstein had to admit. Now though there is still no real consensus of scientists on this issue, but one theory that seems to me to make the most sense out of the particle-wave experimental findings is called Quantum Field Theory (QFT) - which says that "there is no such a thing as a particle" (from <u>Fields of Color: The Theory that Escaped Einstein</u>, by Rodney Brooks). [though no less than Stephen Hawking seems to describe it all in terms of particles, or "virtual particles" in <u>A Brief History of Time</u>]

And now scientists tell us that 95% of everything which really exists in the universe is invisible, apparently immaterial, such that it cannot be observed or measured (has to be mathematically deduced, using computer models) - how does one use the scientific method on something that can't be observed (who needs it when we have computer models?)? Anyway, the point is that scientists tell us they don't even know what 95% of everything is - so they just call it "dark matter" and "dark energy." So if you earned your PhD in Physics in the 20th century guess what? Expert that you may have been, you probably didn't really know what you were probably talking about 20 years ago. Now most physicists agree on one thing - we don't know as much as we thought we did, and there are as many questions as there are answers, if not more.

But one thing most of them are sure of, there aren't any meaningful answers in the Bible, certainly not with respect to the future of our world, of mankind, or of the universe - the Bible is just for religious fanatics. And since these experts know this, and the mainstream media, and our educators in our public schools are telling us that they all agree on this, it is "common knowledge" of our day. Sophisticated educated people that we are, or at least common sense thinkers that we pride ourselves in being, now we know for sure that the Bible is just about religion and faith. But it has no value when it comes to answers about the kind of issues and questions addressed in the first chapter - what in the world is going on, and where are we going?

One little question, we know this about the Bible because …? Because we have looked into it, informed ourselves about what it says, and critically examined its relevance, reliability and accuracy on such subjects? These scientist that know so much about the Bible, have they studied it too, or how many have even read it? Have they put any effort into reading the prophetic book of Daniel, or Revelation, such that they can honestly give an informed opinion on it? Of course they are so smart, and know so much about everything that they now have to admit they may have been consistently wrong about such basic things as the universe being made of discrete particles, and don't really have very definitive answers about the most basic questions - more questions than answers, and this in the areas which they have studied exhaustively. Yet something they haven't had the time of day for, they are now experts on anyway? And now they would have us to believe that everybody and anybody with any brains knows that Bible prophecy is the stuff of religious fanatics, or just a matter of faith - not much reality or relevance. What is wrong with this picture?

Ok, enough of this sarcasm, lets get to the point. In this chapter we will address just a few of the more significant facts to make a point. We will take a look at what the Bible had predicted in the past, and whether or not it passes the validation test (which too many scientific models today aren't even subjected to - including all of the climate-change models). Did the ancient prophets get it right back then. Are they getting it right still today?

Is Bible Prophecy Really Relevant Today?

It really doesn't take a rocket scientist, or a brain surgeon, or a PhD, or even a Theologian to find the answers to these questions. Admittedly a casual reading of the source document, the Bible, will not magically explain everything. It does take some disciplined research into the subject matter - some study of the material, some objective critical thinking, some putting together pieces to come up with a picture that makes sense - and did I mention **Critical Thinking**? Then it takes a fair amount of work at matching the picture that emerges from Bible prophecy, with historic and even current events.

Furthermore reading what men have written, or listening to their explanations and theories may also be less than satisfying, possibly even counterproductive. There are admittedly many diverse interpretations and theories which are neither really scriptural nor logical - don't pass the critical thinking test. Many have already proven to be off-track, or are being proven to be quite inaccurate as the future moves into the past. One example is the popular "revived Roman Empire Theory," which sees the European Union (EU), or European Common Market (ECM) as becoming the coalition of nations which form the end-times beast of Revelation and Daniel, with the global dictator or world ruler called the Antichrist being the president or leader of that European coalition. Such an interpretation is looking more and more unlikely and unbelievable every day, and keeps people from seeing what indeed is a rather obvious fulfillment of those prophecies. But it also fails the critical thinking test with respect to actual literal biblical substantiation - in fact it seems to contradict literal prophetic scripture.

The Bible is actually full of prophetic passages. Much if not most of those prophetic passages find their fulfillment in events that are now part of the record of history. But there is still a significant portion that has not yet been fulfilled and hence are presumed to be about the future. Some of those unfulfilled prophecies, or predictions, are in fact being fulfilled before our eyes. Of course not all of those who claim to be believers and even Bible scholars are on the same page about Bible prophecy. Some even insist that almost all of what is prophesied has already been fulfilled. However, their approach to interpretation of the Bible is incredibly inconsistent, taking quite literally the parts that clearly have already been literally fulfilled, then taking an allegorical approach to the rest. While they say that prophecies about the rise and fall of Egypt and Babylon and the Medo-Persian and Alexandrian Empires are literally fulfilled, those that go on to predict a global holocaust and cosmic disasters are just hyperbolic (i.e. grossly exaggerated) poetic literature and were fulfilled in AD 70 when the Romans destroyed tiny Jerusalem and the temple. It is amazing how many very intelligent and knowledgeable Bible scholars have bought into this Historicists or Preterist view. But admittedly it made more sense in Origin's and Augustine's day and even Calvin's day, when there was no nation Israel, since so many of those prophecies are focused on the nation Israel.

However, this brings us to one of those pervasive aspects of Bible prophecy, which is in itself evidence with respect to which view makes more sense - that the focus of most of that prophecy is on the Middle-East with Israel at the epicenter. For most of two millennia, over 1800 years, there was no nation of Israel. The Romans under the Caesar Vespasian and his son and general Titus, demolished Jerusalem and the temple there in AD 70. She was not even a Jewish homeland until the late 19th century when the Zionists movement, largely inspired by Theodor Herzl, and led by Chaim Weizmann, resulted in the British Balfour Declaration in 1917 which endorsed the creation of a Jewish homeland in Palestine, which was adopted by the League of Nations in 1922. She did not again become a recognized nation until the mid 20th century - 1948 to be exact.

During that time it seemed that either such biblical prophecies were just religious fantasy, or they were written in such symbolic or allegorical language not much could be taken literally, including all references to Israel, and Jerusalem. It became popular for Christians who believed in the Bible, to interpret it all so symbolically that even what we find in Revelation was to find fulfillment in the early church era, in AD 70, in the age of Nero, or Diocletian. Still today such interpretations are prominent among Reformed Theologians. But with the emergence of Israel as a people back in her biblical homeland, and now as an actual state, at center stage on the world scene, Bible scholars are coming back to a more consistent approach to interpretation, which is much less amenable and susceptible to speculation. We now see that in fact just as the earlier prophecies are taken literally, especially in the book of Daniel, it actually makes more sense to take it all equally literally.

However, for the skeptic who prefers to write it all off as religious nonsense, there is a rational question which demands a rational answer. How could anyone have predicted the present situation with the nation Israel such a focus of attention, and such a major player in global politics, always at the center of world attention? What were the odds back in AD 90 when John wrote Revelation, that Israel would even be in existence, let alone that "holy city" of Jerusalem, with a "temple of God" there (see Revelation 11:1-2).

Aha - a gotcha. There is no temple there. Furthermore it doesn't look like a temple being built there on the Temple Mount could ever be a possibility without a major war with the Muslims. Again, ignorance of facts, and the misconceptions of common knowledge strikes. This will be answered in the following, but is addressed thoroughly in a book by Robert Cornuke, <u>Temple - Amazing New Discoveries That Change Everything About the Location of Solomon's Temple</u>.

But we can go back much further. Although there are relevant predictions in many of the books of prophecy as well as other biblical passages, they mostly appear in the major prophets of Isaiah, Jeremiah, Ezekiel and Daniel, and then Revelation in the New Testament. Since this is not primarily a book just on Bible prophecy (as are other books written by this author), we will limit our discussion to a few examples, mostly found in the book of Daniel and the book of Revelation.

Daniel's Prophecies Already Fulfilled - Predictions that Proved to be Accurate

Daniel lived in the time of the historic Babylonian Empire and witnessed its fall to the Med-Persian Empire (that would be the 7th-6th centuries BC). In fact he predicted the rise and fall not only of those empires, but others that followed them. Now skeptics have tried to disqualify this quite astounding feat by claiming that the prophecies of Daniel were not really written by Daniel, certainly not before they happened, but much later by a Macabean after many of them happened, as in the 2nd century BC. However, their arguments have been soundly refuted, and they have nothing but speculation with respect to their imagined author, with absolutely no evidence to support their claims. Finding most of the book of Daniel in the Dead Sea scrolls have contributed to the credibility of the claims of biblical apologists for the earlier dates. Futhermore, even the later dates do not account for all of the prophecies appearing in Daniel. But even if it did we have the internal evidence of the rest of the Bible which would all have to be thrown out. Daniel is mentioned as a prophet by Ezekiel, and by Jesus in the Gospel according to Matthew (Matthew 24:15) where Jesus quoted from Daniel in reference to end-times prophecy. Then we have the witness of the early secular historian Josephus, and the apocryphal book of 1 Maccabees. In addition to that the book of Daniel appears in the Greek version of the Old Testament known as the Septuagint, which we know was written between 280 and 180 BC - which still precedes the second century BC dates when Daniel's detailed prophecy about Antiochus IV Epiphanes was fulfilled. So what we have is the speculative theories of skeptics who don't want to believe that God revealed things to a man named Daniel, with no evidence to support their claims. That is set against a considerable amount of evidence to refute their claims and support the Bible's own claims for itself - God revealed these things to Daniel by supernatural divine revelation. Some of us choose to go with the actual evidence.

So what did Daniel predict? In the second chapter of Daniel he interpreted a dream by King Nebuchadnezzar of the Babylonian Empire. In that dream Nebuchadnezzar saw a huge image of a man, with a head of gold, breast and arms of silver, belly and thighs of bronze, its legs of iron, and its feet (with ten toes) of iron mixed with clay. That image was then crushed by huge stone *carved out of the mountain without hands,*" (Daniel 2:45), and it crushed the whole image all at one time. That stone them became a great mountain which filled the whole earth.

Daniel interpreted it as predicting Nebuchadnezzar's rise to world domination, as well as the fall of his empire. He predicted that it would be replaced by another empire, and that by another, and then another, and finally a last great world empire. But they all would be destroyed once for all by "the God of heaven," who would set up His kingdom on this earth, which would last forever. Other than the first empire which is identified as Babylon, the others were not named in this second chapter, though they were identified in pursuing chapters and we do know from history who they were.

But Daniel didn't stop there. The next time, recorded in the seventh chapter, it was a dream Daniel had initially involving four beasts. Again, they were very symbolic, using a winged lion, a bear, a winged leopard, and then a beast with ten horns, teeth of iron and claws of bronze. Daniel explains that they represent four rulers of four successive kingdoms. That fourth beast then actually consists of ten kings or nations, but then another horn rises up to become dominant over the ten as a fifth ruler, and replaces three of the original ten horns. Again we can know from history who the first three were, but Daniel didn't really identify them yet in this seventh chapter. If Daniel had stopped there these prophecies would be more like Nostradamus or Edgar Cayce type of prophecies - vague enough that we could not really call them accurate predictions, or evidence for supernatural revelation. But again, Daniel did not stop there. In fact he was just getting on a roll.

In the eighth chapter he again relates a vision about the future from his perspective. This vision started with a ram with two horns, but one horn, which was originally smaller, grew to be the larger one. But this ram was then attacked and soundly defeated by a "male goat" with a large horn between his eyes. No one could stand against this male goat, but then somehow the large horn was broken, and four horns came up in its place, one from each of the four corners of the earth.

Now anyone who is at all familiar with ancient history will probably recognize what these symbols represent in terms of actual historical empires. However, we don't have to guess at who Daniel was talking about in these predictions in this eighth chapter, because this time he explicitly names them. He tells us that "*the ram with two horns represents **the kings of Media and Persia**"* (Daniel 8:20). According to what he wrote this prediction was being made while Babylon was still the reigning empire with Belshazzar as the king. Then he goes on to tell us exactly who that male goat with the large horn represents: "*And the large horn represents **the kingdom of Greece**, and the large horn that is between his eyes is the first king*" (Daniel 8:21). Here we have two very specific prophecies or predictions that were exactly accurate, which we now know from history. While the first happened in Daniel's lifetime (6th century BC), the second about Alexander the Great didn't happen until several centuries later (4th century BC).

These interpretations by Daniel also make it clear what the other preceding prophecies were about in the second and seventh chapters of Daniel as we have a clear correlation between them. Starting with the head of the image in chapter two, which correlates to the winged lion of chapter seven, we know that it is Babylon and King Nebuchadnezzar. Then we have the Medo-Persian take over which correlates to the silver shoulders of that image of chapter two, which also correlates to the Bear of chapter seven. The bear is raising up on one side which correlates to the Persians becoming dominant over the Medes, a fact of history. That in turn correlates to the ram with the two horns in chapter eight, the one becoming dominant, representing also the Persian Empire's ascendancy to dominance. However, the ram is violently defeated by the "male goat," or the "shaggy goat," which correlates to the third empire of the image of chapter two, the bronze belly and thighs, which in turn correlates to the winged leopard of chapter seven. So we know that Daniel was writing about that Greek Empire of Alexander the Great, as he tells us in this eighth chapter.

Now exactly as Daniel predicted, the Alexandrian Empire became divided between his four generals, symbolized by *"four conspicuous horns toward the four winds of heaven"* (Daniel 8:8), when he died quite prematurely. They were Cassandra who took the Western part (Greece), Lysimachus who took the Northern part (Asia Minor), Seleucus who took the Eastern part (Syria and Israel), and Ptolemy who took the Southern part (Egypt). Then Daniel goes on to describe a king that will come from one of those four horns using the symbology of the *"small horn"* again, just as he did in the symbology of the last beast of the seventh chapter - the one with ten horns. And here again this description also matches that of the *"little horn"* of the seventh chapter. So again we have a correlation, which lets us know that he is talking about the same thing in each chapter just using different symbols, except that in this case he is even using the same symbol of the little horn.

Similarly there is the correlation of the image of the second chapter, which has feet with ten toes, which corresponds to the ten horns of the fourth beast of chapter seven. For this beast however, we find no complete fulfillment in history - though we do see partial fulfillment of the "little horn" in the person of Antiochus IV Epiphanes. It makes sense that they are not completely fulfilled, since they are both the final kingdoms that are destroyed by none other than God Himself, which Daniel also tells us is about *"the time of the end"* (8:17 & 19), and *"many days in the future"* (8:29).

There is indeed much debate between Bible scholars as to what the "legs of iron" of the image in the second chapter represents, some insisting it is Rome, as in the Roman Empire, others arguing it is the later Islamic empire. The Roman Empire did follow the Greek Empire, but did not really control the same regions, except for the eastern Mediterranean region that included Israel - and that not until the middle of the first century BC. However, in Daniel's other prophecies in chapters seven and following, there really is no mention of the Roman Empire, but a strong focus on the Ptolemaic and Seleucid line of kings down to Antiochus IV Epiphanes, which Rome never conquered. That line, including the Middle-East and Egypt of today, eventually became subsumed under the Islamic Empires, The Ottoman Turks having conquered the last vestige of the old Roman Empire in 1453, which had become the Byzantine Empire (the Eastern Roman Empire). But for purposes of this discussion that is all a rather mute point, not very relevant.

What is relevant is that Daniel goes on in the ninth chapter to actually give us a timeline, 70 weeks of years or 490 years (Daniel consistently uses the term *"weeks"* to refer to periods of seven years), and gives a specific starting point - *"a decree to restore and rebuild Jerusalem"* (Daniel 9:24-25). We know from history, and from scripture (Ezra 1:1-4 & 6:3-5), that Cyrus the king of Persia issued such a decree, which was dated at 450 BC (though admittedly this is debated among scholars). He then tells us that in the first seven weeks of years, 49 years, Jerusalem would be rebuilt. Then there would be 62 more weeks, or 434 years until *"the Messiah will be cut off"* (Daniel 9:26). Hence Daniel predicted that there would be 483 years between the time of Cyrus' decree to rebuild Jerusalem, and the time Jesus, the Messiah, would be "cut off." Jesus is believed to have died at age 33, so we have from 450 BC to 0 BC (which was also AD 1) = 450 years, plus 33 years = exactly 483 years. [These calculations assume Jesus was born in AD 1, or 0 BC, which is not known for sure. Other's start with a date of 444 BC but believe Christ was born in AD 6, still giving us 483 years.]

Now what person in their right mind would say that Daniel, living in the sixth century BC could have predicted to the exact year (some have calculated it down to a precise day) when Jesus the Messiah would die, over 600 years later - without something a little supernatural going on? Even if we were to allow the late dates set by the skeptics for the authorship of Daniel, 164-167 BC, it was still a precise prediction by whoever wrote it almost

200 years before Christ's prophesied death (which really only speaks to the inadequacy of their alternative explanations).

So up to this point we have three historic empires explicitly named, with precise predictions about their emergence and demise, and we have precise times given to the year predicting when Christ the Messiah would die - "be cut off." At this point for any half-way objective reasonable person, I should be able to rest my case. The evidence is more than enough to prove in a court of law that the Bible's claims and Daniel's claims to be giving us supernatural divine revelations from God, were in fact just that. But there is more, much more.

Daniel then goes on in the eleventh chapter to give us detailed predictions of what would transpire in that region around Israel. He focuses on two of the four kingdoms which came out of the Greek empire, which he calls the King of the North, and the King of the South. Again, it doesn't take that much to determine who Daniel, or God, had in mind, when we look at the historic record. Historically there were ongoing struggles between the Seleucid line - the Syrian kingdom, and the Ptolemaic line - the Egyptian kingdom. Here we have an account of specific rulers and their struggles and how they came to power, and battles between them. The following are a few examples of what he accurately predicted, all of which are a matter of historic record, up through at least the 35th verse of that eleventh chapter.

Daniel wrote: *"After some years they will form an alliance, and the daughter of the king of the South will come to the king of the North to carry out a peaceful arrangement. But she will not retain her position of power, nor will he remain with his power, but she will be given up, along with those who brought her in and the one who sired her as well as he who supported her in those times."* (Daniel 11:6)

The historic record: An alliance between Antiochus II Theos and Ptolemy II Philadelphus involving the latter's daughter, Berenice, which was given to Antiochus as his wife; but he had to first divorce his own wife Laodicea; but when Ptolemy II died Antiochus took Laodicea back, who then murdered both Antiochus and Berenice and her son.

Daniel wrote: *"But one of the descendants of her line will arise in his place, and he will come against their army and enter the fortress of the king of the North, and he will deal with them and display great strength. ⁸Also their gods with their metal images and their precious vessels of silver and gold he will take into captivity to Egypt, and he on his part will refrain from attacking the king of the North for some years."* (Daniel 11:7-8)
History: Loadicea's brother, Ptolemy III Euergetes then prevailed militarily over the North's Seleucus Callinicus (246-221 BC), taking back captives ("princes" as hostages) and spoil to Egypt.

Daniel wrote: *"He will set his face to come with the power of his whole kingdom, bringing with him a proposal of peace which he will put into effect; he will also give him the daughter of women to ruin it. But she will not take a stand for him or be on his side."* (Daniel 11:17)
History: A peace treaty when, under pressure from Rome the King of the North, Antiochus III, strategically gave his daughter, Cleopatra I, to marry seven year old Ptolemy V Epiphanes (circa 192 BC) - but she sided with her husband against her father.

From the twenty-first through the thirty-fifth verse we have prophecies, or predictions that are mostly about one which Daniel calls *"**a despicable person**."* We find that Daniel gives an incredibly detailed account of what we know Antiochus IV Epiphanes did, several centuries after Daniel was dead, taking us down to 165 BC. Here is a brief rendition going verse by verse through Daniel 11:20-35.
Daniel wrote: *"Then in his place one will arise who will send an oppressor through the Jewel of his kingdom; yet within a few days he will be shattered, though not in anger nor in battle. In his place a despicable person will arise, on whom the honor of kingship has not been conferred, but he will come in a time of tranquility and seize the kingdom by intrigue."* (Daniel 11:21)

History: Antiochus IV Epiphanes came to power illegitimately and fraudulently through deception and chicanery. When the ruler Seleucus IV, his brother died, he posed as the guardian of his brother's young son also name Antiochus, who was the legal heir, but instead actually secured the throne for himself. Mysteriously his nephew, the legal heir, was murdered (probably part of his plot).

Daniel wrote: *"The overflowing forces will be flooded away before him and shattered, and also the prince of the covenant."* (v. 22)

History: Antiochus defeated Heliodorus after driving Egypt out of Syria, and invading Egypt to Memphis; then he captured Ptolemy Philometer whom he tried to use to gain control of Egypt. He also had Onais the governing high priest in Jerusalem (*"the prince of the covenant"*), executed.

**Daniel wrote: *"He will stir up his strength and courage against the king of the South with a large army; so the king of the South will mobilize an extremely large and mighty army for war; but he will not stand, for schemes will be devised against him. 26Those who eat his choice food will destroy him, and his army will overflow, but many will fall down slain."* (vv. 25-26)

History: Philometer and Physcon raised a large army to drive the Syrians out of Egypt, but end up fighting each other resulting in Antiochus invading Egypt down to Alexandria - but he failed to take Alexandria.

Daniel wrote: *"Then he will return to his land with much plunder; but his heart will be set against the holy covenant, and he will take action and then return to his own land."* (v. 28)

History: Antiochus returns to Jerusalem on his way back from Egypt to Antioch and plunders the temple and the city.

Daniel wrote: *"At the appointed time he will return and come into the South, but this last time it will not turn out the way it did before. 30For ships of Kittim will come against him; therefore he will be disheartened and will return and become* *enraged at the holy covenant and take action; so he will come back and show regard for those who forsake the holy covenant."* (vv. 29-30)

History: Antiochus tried to invade Egypt again in 168 BC (v. 29) but was forced to withdraw by Roman consul, Gaius Popillius Laenas ("the ships of Kittim" v. 30).

Returning from Egypt in a rage Antiochus returns to Jerusalem, supports a Jewish Priest named Jason (172 BC), a reform party Jew who was committed to Hellenization of Judaism (*"those who forsake the holy covenant"*); Antiochus then appoints Menelaus to replace Jason, but Jason retakes Jerusalem by force murdering many of his opponents. (v. 30)

Daniel wrote: *"Forces from him will arise, desecrate the sanctuary fortress, and do away with the regular sacrifice. And they will set up the abomination of desolation."* (v. 31)

History: Antiochus sent Appolonius (June 167 BC) who desecrated the altar in the temple by sacrificing a pig, set up an altar to Zeus Olympius, and an image of Antiochus as an idol to be worshipped as God - the "**abomination of desolation**," and put a stop to daily sacrifices.

Daniel wrote: *"By smooth words he will turn to godlessness those who act wickedly toward the covenant, but the people who know their God will display strength and take action. 33Those who have insight among the people will give understanding to the many; yet they will fall by sword and by flame, by captivity and by plunder for many days. 34Now when they fall they will be granted a little help, and many will join with them in hypocrisy. 35Some of those who have insight will fall, in order to refine, purge and make them pure until the end time; because it is still to come at the appointed time."* (vv. 32-35)

History: The Maccabean revolt (December164 BC) ended the 3½ year reign of terror of Antiochus IV Epiphanes - liberated Jerusalem, restored the sanctuary and the sacrificial system (vv. 32-35). Some of the Jews became somewhat Hellenized and joined the forces of Antiochus against their brothers, but the other Jews resisted valiantly, first led by Jason who overthrew Menelaus. But they were again defeated by Antiochus' forces. That was followed by the revolt of the Maccabeans, faithful Jews who successfully retook the city and rebuilt the temple, established the Hasmonean dynasty and maintained an independent Jewish state for about a century, until the Roman General, Pompey the Great subjugated them in 63 BC.

Now what we have here in Daniel is only a few examples of **over 100, some count approximately 135 prophetic statements, which have all already been fulfilled. How foolish is it to ignore this kind of predictive accuracy**? Of course, as the Bible also says, "*The fool has said in his heart there is no God*" (Psalm 14:1 & 53:1). As Paul wrote to the Romans, "*Professing to be wise they became fools*" (Romans 1:22). This is one of those areas in which a certain amount of arrogance combined with ignorance seems to be allowing people, who may be very intelligent and even knowledgeable, as well as the ignorant masses, to actually be quite irrational in their choices with respect to what they believe and don't believe.

Chapter 3 What Does the Bible Actually Predict About the Future?

Up to this point we have looked at predictions made by just one of the ancient Prophets found in the Bible, Daniel. We have only looked at those prophecies or predictions that have already proven to be quite accurate such that they are now matters of ancient history. They extend from the days of Nebuchadnezzar and his Babylonian Empire, down to Antiochus IV Epiphanes and the succeeding Maccabean revolt and the establishment of the Hasmonean Dynasty in Israel. However, Daniel's predictions do not stop there. And where Daniel leaves off, John picks up with his prophetic book of Revelation.   Like Daniel, John predicts developments that have already happened even in recent time. His prophecies are very much overlapping and connected with, and obviously correlated to Daniel's prophecies, such that even some of the same symbology is used by both.

Daniel's Predictions That Haven't Happened Yet
In Daniel's prophecy in the second chapter of the book by his name, we saw the image of a man, with a head of gold, breast and arms of silver, belly and thighs of bronze, legs of iron, and feet of iron mixed with clay. In the previous chapter (of this book) we saw that by matching this image up with what is explained in the seventh and eighth chapters of Daniel we know that Daniel was predicting four successive empires, which have come and gone already. The gold head Daniel himself interpreted as Nebuchadnezzar's Babylonian Empire. The silver breast and arms was the Medo-Persian Empire, which succeeded the Babylonian without destroying it. Then we had the belly and thighs of bronze, which was the Grecian Empire of Alexander the Great, which conquered much of the former Babylonian and Medo-Persian Empires. After that we had a period during which most of Mesopotamia, or the former Alexandrian Grecian Empire was ruled by the descendants of two of the four Generals who inherited Alexander's empire,

Seleucid and Ptolemy. The descendents of these two battled between themselves for centuries.

Meanwhile Rome came on the scene and the Roman Empire included the western parts of those old Empires, including parts of Syria and Egypt and Palestine, or Israel. For that reason many Bible scholars have interpreted the legs of iron to be representing the old Roman Empire. Others however today believe that it was the Moslem or Islamic Empire as the better fulfillment of this prophecy. That Islamic empire initially conquered the Byzantine Romans in Jerusalem in AD 636, and all of Syria by 641, and the entire Grecian Empire by AD 1453. It also included most of the same territory geographically, hence most of the same nations, people groups and cultures, as were included under the Babylonian, Medo-Persian and Grecian empires - much more so than did the Roman Empire.

Furthermore the fact is that we don't see any prophetic reference to Ancient Rome or the Roman Empire through the rest of Daniel's prophecies (though some believe it appears in Daniel 9:26 - which is a problematic interpretation at best). But there does seem to be a better match to the Islamic Empires still prevalent today in the Mesopotamian area. Thus perhaps the latter is likely the better interpretation.* However, the main point here is that there is still part of this image - the feet of iron and clay, which we do not find already fulfilled in history. *[A number of authors have addressed this issue dealing with the popular Revived Roman Empire theory. At least two recent books are primarily dealing with this subject, both demonstrating considerable research and knowledge on the subject and reaching very similar conclusions. They are <u>Daniel Revisited</u> by Mark Davidson, and <u>The Coming Bible Prophecy Reformation</u> by Rodrigo Silva.]

If we understand the legs of iron of this image as representing the Islamic Empire (Caliphates), we have some continuity from the Alexandrian Empire, through the Seleucid Dynasty (centered in Syria), down through the Islamic Empire - in particular the Ottoman Empire - to our present day. In that case it would make sense to see the feet of the image as an extension or an outgrowth of the legs of iron, as Islam is very much still a very prominent and powerful presence in that region today, even though it is not what it used to be in the days of the Ottoman Empire. Unlike the previous Empires, including the Roman Empire, the Islamists crushed the other empires she conquered (with some exceptions), by changing their native religions (to Islam), their languages (to Arabic) and their laws (to Sharia Law). However, what we have seen going on in the Middle-East today is an even more literal crushing of her enemies as Al Qaeda, ISIS (or IS of ISIL), and numerous other Islamic terrorist organizations, have massacred men, women and children, and destroyed historic landmarks. This correlates well to the fourth beast in the seventh chapter, which in Daniel's prophetic vision *"devoured and crushed and trampled down the remainder with its feet"* (Daniel 7:7 & 19), and according to his prediction *"will be different from all the other kingdoms and will devour the whole earth and tread it down and crush it."* (Daniel 7:23b). That is not to say that any of these recent and current forms such as ISIS, are themselves that beast, but they are just recent forms of that evolving beast.

What we see then is some kind of a "kingdom" which is represented by two feet, and ten toes. This is predicted by Daniel to be the last kingdom that will exist in this world, as it will be destroyed by what Daniel calls *"a stone* [that] *was cut out without hands"* (Daniel 2:34 - i.e. not man-made as in modern weapons of mass destruction). According to Daniel's prediction, this "stone" will crush the feet - that last kingdom. However, it will not only crush the feet, but the whole image, which means that **all the other preceding empires of that image will be present in some form, but will be completely obliterated at that time**. Furthermore, he is prophesying that in their place will be a kingdom established which would last forever. The symbology used is that the very stone that crushes the other kingdoms will itself become a mountain, which will fill the whole earth (Daniel 2:35). One might begin to get the idea that this is as an "end-of-the-world-as-we-know-it" scenario, a "doomsday" scenario for many earth-dwellers. On the other hand, it sounds like a solution, logically the only solution, to the present day dilemma we face today, as addressed in the opening chapter of this book - a future world government replacing all the warring factions around the globe today - no more terrorism, no more war.

To find out for sure what Daniel meant by this future, not yet fulfilled part, we have to stay tuned - keep reading. He goes on in the seventh chapter to explain what he meant in the second chapter, about the stone that crushes the feet. There in chapter seven we see three beasts, which as discussed in the preceding chapter represent three empires again, which also correspond to three of the empires predicted in the second chapter. We have a winged lion, which like the gold head of the image represents the **Babylonian Empire**. This is followed by a bear with three ribs in its mouth, raised up on one side. This corresponds to the silver arms and breast of the image, and is interpreted for us in the next chapter of Daniel (8:20) as being the **Medo-Persian Empir**e - Persia becoming the dominant power. That is followed by the winged leopard, which had four wings and four heads, which again correlates to the bronze belly and thighs of the image. And again it is interpreted for us in the eighth chapter as being the **Grecian, or Alexandrian Empire** and its division into four smaller kingdoms under Alexander's four generals (Cassander, Lysimachus, Ptolemy, and Seleucus). **This part is now history - accurate predictions made by Daniel that have already been fulfilled**.

But Daniel goes on to prophesy about another kingdom, or progression of kingdoms, using the imagery of a *"dreadful,"* *"terrifying"* and *"extremely strong"* beast, with large iron teeth and bronze claws and ten heads. Whoa - ten horns? Ok, first a winged lion, then a four-winged four-headed leopard, but now a ten-horned beast? Could there be something significant about this number ten? Could it relate to the ten toes of the feet of the image? Of course it does, and we will see that it is a theme which is carried out through not only Daniel's prophecy but the Apostle John explains it further in his revelations in - what else, the book of Revelation (Revelation 12:3, 13:1, 17:3).

But we are not through yet with this final beast. Daniel tells us that another horn - a *"little horn"* - springs up amongst the ten. Then three of the other ten are uprooted, leaving only seven horns. This horn is identified as a man with a big mouth -

"uttering great boasts" (Daniel 7:8), and it becomes *"larger"* than its associates - apparently becoming the most powerful, the leader of this coalition of ten nations.

In Daniel's next chapter, the eighth chapter (Daniel 8:9-12), we again see this little *"little horn"* described. It is coming from the four horns of a *"male goat"* or *"shaggy goat,"* which we are told in 8:21 is the Grecian Empire - the four horns obviously symbolizing the four divisions between Alexander's generals after he died. Then we are told that from one of the four divisions of this kingdom, *"in the latter period of their rule … a king will arise, insolent and skilled in intrigue"* (8:22-23). This is the explanation that corresponds to the previous symbolic prediction about the *"small horn"* in verses 9-12 (of that eighth chapter). What is so interesting and significant about these predictions is that they are a mixed bag of fulfilled and not yet fulfilled prophecies. Obviously the part about the destruction of this beast, the annihilation of his kingdom, and the establishment of the kingdom in which God and His people (*"the people of the saints of the Highest One"* - Daniel 7:27) will be in power and reign forever - hasn't happened yet. In light of the accuracy of all the other predictions, what are the odds that it is going to happen?

We also haven't really seen such a powerful empire that is made up of a coalition of ten nations, which is reduced to seven nations once a powerful ruler rises to power over them. This ruler is described more in the eighth and eleventh chapters of Daniel, and then again in the book of Revelation. The following is what Daniel wrote in those two following chapters:

*"21The shaggy goat represents the kingdom of Greece, and the large horn that is between his eyes is the first king. 22The broken horn and the four horns that arose in its place represent four kingdoms which will arise from his nation, although not with his power. 23 In the latter period of their rule, when the transgressors have run their course, **a king will arise**, insolent and skilled in intrigue. 24 His power will be mighty, but not by his own power, and he will destroy to an extraordinary degree and prosper and perform his will; he will destroy mighty men and the holy people. 25 And*

*through his shrewdness He will cause deceit to succeed by his influence; and he will magnify himself in his heart, and he will destroy many while they are at ease. He will **even oppose the Prince of princes**, but he will be **broken without human agency**." (Daniel 8:21-25)*

*[36]Then the king will do as he pleases, and he will exalt and magnify himself above every god and will speak monstrous things against the God of gods; and he will prosper until the indignation is finished, for that which is decreed will be done. [37]He will **show no regard for the gods of his fathers or for the desire of women, nor will he show regard for any other god**; for he will magnify himself above them all. [38]But instead **he will honor a god of fortresses, a god whom his fathers did not know; he will honor him with gold, silver, costly stones and treasures.** [39]He will **take action against the strongest of fortresses with the help of a foreign god**; he will give great honor to those who acknowledge him and will cause them to rule over the many, and will parcel out land for a price.*
*[40]At the **end time** the king of the South will collide with him, and the king of the North will storm against him with chariots, with horsemen and with many ships; and he will enter countries, overflow them and pass through. [41]He will also **enter the Beautiful Land**, and many countries will fall; but these will be rescued out of his hand: **Edom, Moab** and the foremost of the sons of **Ammon**. [42]Then he will stretch out his hand against other countries, and the land of **Egypt will not escape**. [43]But he will gain control over the hidden treasures of gold and silver and over all the precious things of Egypt; and **Libyans and Ethiopians will follow at his heels**. [44]But rumors from the East and from the North will disturb him, and he will go forth with great wrath to destroy and annihilate many. [45]He will pitch the tents of his royal pavilion **between the seas and the beautiful Holy Mountain**; yet he will come to his end, and no one will help him." (Daniel 11:36-46)*

Part of what we see described in these passages seems to match Antiochus IV Epiphanes and his exploits (as we saw in the previous chapter), but then it goes beyond what he did. When Daniel speaks of the Prince of Princes He is referring to no less than the incarnation of God, which was of course Jesus Christ. This powerful ruler is said to actually come into a confrontation with God in the form of Jesus Christ, who ultimately defeats him. That is why Daniel writes that he will be destroyed or broken, without human agency. The historic Antiochus was leading most of his army to fight against the Parthians, when he died of some disease. Though the Maccabees were revolting in Jerusalem, he actually sent a contingent with his general Lysias to put down the uprising. This is not what Daniel prophesied about the King who would arise in that eighth chapter. Either he got it wrong for the first time, or he was predicting something that hasn't happened yet. When we go on to see what else he wrote about it, we see that he was writing about something that he says isn't to happen until *"the end time"* (Daniel 11:40). And this is how he introduced his explanation of this whole prophecy in chapter eight: *"Behold, I am going to let you know what will occur at **the final period** of the indignation, for **it pertains to the appointed time of the end.***" (Daniel 8:19).

In the eleventh chapter we see this same king described in the eighth chapter, where he is being called the King of the North. Up to that 36th verse we see description of events in amazing detail, which have already become part of the record of history, much of it fulfilled in the historic Antiochus IV Epiphanes of the mid second century BC. Starting with that 36th verse there are some features of this king Daniel is describing which seem to match Antiochus, but others that don't, and progressively more so as the prophecy continues. Since Daniel tells us that he is writing about the appointed time of the end, it make more sense to understand this as something that is not in the history books because it is about the future - hasn't happened yet.

Bible scholars who have studied Bible prophecy tell us that there is this technique used in scripture that involves what they call **dual prophecy**. The duality is the fact that what the prophets wrote had immediate value to the audiences of their time in that there was a near term aspect with respect to their fulfillment - they were predicting things that would happen in their own lifetimes, or within a few generations. What Daniel predicted about Babylon and Medo-Persia coming to power, happened in his lifetime. Much of what else he wrote happened within a few centuries of when he wrote it (about 530 BC to 165 BC). Along with other prophets, most notably Isaiah and Jeremiah and Ezekiel, what they prophesied had meaning and value to the Jews of their time as it involved warnings as well as reassuring promises, to which they needed to pay heed. However, in many if not most of these prophecies was also embedded a long range prophecy, with features that would not find fulfillment until the end of time, or as Daniel also calls it, the "last days." One of the powerful internal evidences for the Bible being divine revelation supernaturally inspired by God, is this fact that not only was God telling His people about what to expect in their future, but at the same time was giving us all a glimpse into His overall plan for this world. The long-range view takes us up to the time when He would step in and make it all good again, the way He created it in the first place.

What we see in these passages in Daniel are just more good examples of this dualistic nature of Bible prophecy. Up to a point it has already been fulfilled in amazing detail, but then the long range portion is not to be found in the annals of history - because it is still future. So Daniel tells us that this king who is still to come will in many ways be like Antiochus IV Epiphanes - hence he is called a prototype of that one who is still to come. Of course the one we are talking about is what Bible believers refer to as "the Antichrist."

One might ask, why this dual prophecy business, why not just tell us about that main guy that is coming some day? I see two logical reasons for why God would do it this way. First, the near term aspects of this prophecy give us something to test it by. The amazing accuracy of the part that has been fulfilled should get the attention of the non-believers, that it is reliable and must be coming from a supernatural source (which we call

God). Beyond that it fosters a lot of confidence in the rational believer, that what else He is predicting will also just as surely come to pass just as He says it will. Second, for those who are paying attention, and know what has been predicted, it gives them a lot to look for in that future figure, such that they will recognize it, or him, when he arrives on the scene. And finally, it makes those passages of scripture relevant to everyone who reads them in any age, though for some it pertains to a more distant future than for others.

Beyond that we also learn that there seems to be a circular nature to history. As time goes on and things seem to change so dramatically, we end up coming full circle to where we started - at least going back to the beginning of the post-flood era, and the earliest records of civilization. From the standpoint of secular history, it all began in that Mesopotamian region, the cradle of civilization, with the Sumerian and Akkadian cultures which merged into what became Babylonia. So in a sense it is like a cosmic poetic justice, with man's world coming back to end where it all began - almost like someone in charge of it all knew where it was all going and had a master plan.

In the case of Daniel's prophecies about this future kingdom and its leader, it may not be all that narrowly specific to say that this one that is coming will be a very loud and boastful and deceitful and blasphemous person who will be cruel and vicious and destroy many including God's people Israel. **But all of it taken together, with the part that has been partially fulfilled, gives us a prediction that is in many respects quite precise.** First it tells us where to look for this personality, with respect to his roots and from whence he will come. Second it tells us that he will be re-enacting something that has been done before in Israel, and more specifically to the temple in Jerusalem - that circular pattern mentioned above. Third it tells us "the rest of the story," in which God and His people emerge as the ultimate victors over such evil forces in the world - something we haven't really seen yet in history. In other words, what happened historically is only a chapter in the book of what will ultimately be earth's history. While we know from history that the Maccabees may have driven out the

Syrians (Antiochus' forces) temporarily, they were eventually defeated and slaughtered and their city and temple completely demolished by the Romans in AD 70. Then their land was subjugated to the Islamic invaders, which lasted for over most of the last millennium and a half. But the story doesn't end there, and we see another chapter which is unfolding before our very eyes.

So then what are we looking for such that we can recognize this "Antichrist"? First, he comes from that line of kings, or kingdoms, which originated in the Grecian or Alexandrian Empire, but then became the Seleucid Dynasty, eventually taking us down to Antiochus IV Epiphanes, who was Syrian. We are told that like Antiochus, his forces will desecrate the temple at Jerusalem, and set up ***the abomination of desolation***" in the temple, and he will demand to be worshipped as God. Historians tell us that the Syrians sent by Antiochus desecrated the temple by sacrificing a pig on the altar, and setting up an altar to Zeus Olympius, and an image of himself as an idol to be worshipped. Jesus Himself refers to this in His own prophecy about the last days:

> *"Therefore when you see the **abomination of desolation** which was spoken of through Daniel the prophet, standing in the holy place (let the reader understand), [16]then those who are in Judea must flee to the mountains;" (Matthew 24:15-16).*

In the following we will follow this through other prophetic scriptures down through Revelation to get the whole picture. But first we will note other characteristics given by Daniel by which we can recognize this end-time figure we are calling "the Antichrist."

We see that this character we are looking for will somehow show disregard and disrespect for *"the gods of his fathers ... nor will he show regard for any other god"* (Daniel 11:37). This would seem to indicate that at some point he is going to turn against his own religion, which makes sense if he is going to proclaim himself as being God. If, as we have been leading up to suggesting, this figure is emerging from the Islamic world, it would mean that at some point he claims to be God, or maybe

Allah, which would be going against the Islamic beliefs. Interestingly enough this is what we see that Paul predicts he will do in 2 Thessalonians 2:4, and John predicts in Revelation 17:16, which we will return to later. There is also another possible interpretation for what this prediction could mean, which has to do with the question as to whether this figure may be an ethnic Assyrian - the term used for him in several other prophetic passages. This is also discussed in the following under Other Predictions in the New Testament.

Next we also see in that same verse that he will also disregard *"the desire of women"* (11:37). Now of course men have had a field day with this one with all kinds of far-fetched explanations - such as it was the desire of every Jewish woman to mother the Messiah, so this just means the Antichrist will be anti Christ - which is true but not very helpful. It seems a lot less speculative to just say he won't have much regard or respect for women, or what women want. Does anything come to mind, like maybe a certain prominent Mid-Eastern religion, which subjugates women to the level of possessions owned by men? Could this mean maybe denying women the freedom to dress the way the want to, or to drive a car, or to vote, or to leave an abusive husband, or virtually any other legal rights which their male counterparts enjoy? Hello, has anyone ever heard of Sharia Law? This certainly didn't apply to Rome in which women's liberation was alive and well, nor is it the hallmark of Judaism or Christianity or any of the western cultures.

Next we see that *"he will honor a god of fortresses, a god whom his fathers did not know"* (11:38). Thus he will have the highest regard for "fortresses" - weapons systems and military might - more than for anything else including the god of his fathers' religion. In fact he will spend a considerable amount of wealth on developing those weapons systems, or fortresses, and we see that he will then use them to take action against some formidable opponents, *"the strongest of fortresses with the help of a foreign god"* (11:39). Of course this is pretty wide open as to who the formidable opponents might be - or is it? Who is the whole world watching closely today because they are on the verge of getting nuclear weapons (if they don't have them already - which they probably will by the time this gets published)? Who are they most likely to go after which might be called their "formidable opponents"? Who do they consider their greatest enemy? And what will those enemies really do about it when she gets the nuclear weapons?

Now admittedly what we see next in Daniel's prophecy is pretty obscure - that this Antichrist will enlist the support of *"a foreign god,"* in attacking his enemies. Another rendering of this is: *"And he shall act in the strong holds of the fortresses with a foreign god, whom he shall acknowledge."* (From <u>The Interlinear Hebrew-Aramaic Old Testament</u>, Jay P. Green Sr. as General Editor and Translator, Hendrickson Publishers, Peabody MA, second ed. 1985). Similarly the King James Version reads: *"Thus shall he do in the most strongholds with a strange god, whom he shall acknowledge and increase with glory."* Perhaps when it says a *"strange god"* it means one that is foreign to his own religion, hence he is allying himself with some other god than the god of his fathers (i.e. Allah). It could mean that this emerging world leader is willing to compromise or make concessions to religions other than his own. If he is indeed an Islamists, it may mean that he presents himself on the world stage as a very moderate Islamists, who is not only tolerant of but also embraces other religions. He may seduce the western world by telling them that he believes all religions are true as they are all after all seeking God, however they define Him. This tolerant universalism will include the primary objective of world peace, and he will sell himself as the one who can unite the Moslem and non-Moslem world in a world of peace and shared prosperity. Such a message will be very compatible with the world-wide trend today, at least in the Western world, subscribing to Relativism, and the belief that there are no absolutes, elevating tolerance and peaceful coexistence to the level of a new "golden rule."

Ultimately, as we see from prophecies in the New Testament books, He will set himself up as that God, the Messiah figure for whom the whole world is and looking and waiting - a foreign or strange god indeed to everyone, especially

Islamists. For Islamists this Messiah figure could be their long awaited Mahdi, or Twelfth Imam, until he abandons them and claims to actually be god, in the place of Allah.

Some suggest that it will actually be Satan from whom this Antichrist will get his needed assistance, and whom he will in turn glorify. This sounds too speculative until we get to Revelation where we see the role that "the dragon" - which is identified as Satan - plays in his rise to power.

Daniel goes on to tell us that this leader will be opposed by the *"king of the south"* - which is easily identifiable as Egypt, based on the part that has already been fulfilled. He will invade *"the beautiful land"* which is a biblical term for "Israel." But Edom, Moab and Ammon - which today is mostly in Jordan - will be spared from his conquests for some reason. He will eventually conquer Egypt and take her treasures, and when Egypt falls the North African nations of Libya and Sudan (Daniel's Ethiopia is probably more than likely today's Sudan)* will join him rather than try to oppose him.**

*[According to early Greek writers, Ethiopia was an empire originally situated between Ta-Seti in Lower Kemet and the confluence of the White and Blue Niles. Centuries later, however, the name became synonymous with a much larger region that included the present-day countries of South Sudan, Ethiopia, Eritrea, Djibouti, Somalia, Kenya, Uganda, Central African Republic, Chad, etc (www.taneter.org/ethiopia.html).]

**[According to the Gesenius' Hebrew-Chaldee Lexicon the Hebrew word translated *"will follow* at his heels" in Daniel 11:43, is also rendered "in his footsteps i.e. in his company." Strong gives the following definition: "a step; figuratively, companionship:".]

Then because of disturbing rumors from the East and North, he returns to a location Daniel refers to as *"between the seas and the Holy Mountain."* When we correlate this to other passages describing this event we learn that it is probably referring to the plain of Megiddo and the valley of Esdraelon (in the Hebrew, Plain of Jezreel - a plain in northern Israel which stretches from the Mediterranean near Mt. Carmel to the Jordan River). This is where many famous battles have been fought down through history. This connects it with the "battle of Har Magedon" (or Armageddon) of John's prophecy in Revelation. There this Antichrist meets his "waterloo" so to speak, just as

Napoleon did centuries earlier. Daniel just says there *"he will come to his end, and no one will help him"* (Daniel 11:45b). At this point we have to go to the other passages to get the whole picture with more defining detail.

Other Predictions in the New Testament

There are several New Testament passages that help to paint the picture, and help to interpret for us what Daniel's prophecies are all about. We have alluded to several of them in the preceding discussions, and will address them again here. First we have Paul's prophecy in his letter to the Thessalonians:

*"¹Now we request you, brethren, with regard to the coming of our Lord Jesus Christ and our gathering together to Him, ²that you not be quickly shaken from your composure or be disturbed either by a spirit or a message or a letter as if from us, to the effect that the day of the Lord has come. ³Let no one in any way deceive you, for it will not come unless the apostasy comes first, and **the man of lawlessness is revealed, the son of destruction, ⁴who opposes and exalts himself above every so-called god or object of worship, so that he takes his seat in the temple of God, displaying himself as being God**. ⁵Do you not remember that while I was still with you, I was telling you these things? ⁶And you know what restrains him now, so that in his time he will be revealed. ⁷For the mystery of lawlessness is already at work; only he who now restrains will do so until he is taken out of the way. ⁸Then **that lawless one will be revealed whom the Lord will slay with the breath of His mouth and bring to an end by the appearance of His coming; ⁹that is, the one whose coming is in accord with the activity of Satan, with all power and signs and false wonders,** ¹⁰and with all the deception of wickedness for those who perish, because they did not receive the love of the truth so as to be saved. ¹¹For this reason God will send upon them a deluding influence so that they will believe what is false, ¹²in order that they all may be judged who did not believe*

the truth, but took pleasure in wickedness." (2 Thessalonians 2:1-12 emphasis added)

Here we see Paul predicting that there will be a personage who will appear on the world's stage, sometime before Christ returns to earth to rescue His followers. This one will oppose every other god and set himself up in the temple as being God. This sounds familiar, does it not? Is this not what Daniel was describing in his prophecies about "*the little horn*" of Daniel 7 and 8, the "*king that will arise*" of 8:23-26, the "*despicable person*" of 11:21-45 who will desecrate the temple and set up the "*abomination of desolation*" (11:31). With respect to this "abomination of desolation" Jesus Himself refers to Daniel's prophecy, and lets us know that it is in reference to those end times shortly before He is to return to rescue His own followers from the judgment, which He is going to execute on this earth:

*"Therefore when you see the **abomination of desolation** which was spoken of through Daniel the prophet, standing in the holy place (let the reader understand), ¹⁶then those who are in Judea must flee to the mountains;" (Matthew 24:15-16)*

But of course most of the information that gives us the rest of the story and interprets much of what Daniel wrote, is found in the book of Revelation, also known as "the Apocalypse." There is far more in that book than we can begin to address in this book, much of which is addressed in other books by this author (note)* and many other writers as well. However, we will focus on picking up where Daniel left off, to fill in details and determine the rest of the story, especially as it relates to current global developments, and what would appear to be in our relatively near future.

*[Beginning with a commentary on the whole book of Revelation, The Revelation Revisited, the subject matter has been broken down to be addressed in the following series of books: The Mysteries of Revelation Demystified, The Seals Trumpets and Bowls of Revelation Revisited, The Beast the Antichrist the Harlot Babylon - Popular Theories Revisited and a Sola-Scriptura Proposal, Gog-Magog Revisited, The Millennial Kingdom and The Final Judgments on Earth and the Heavenly New Jerusalem Revisited, and The Pretribulation Rapture Theory and Dispensationalism Revisited.]

We can begin with that strange beast Daniel wrote about, the one with ten horns and a little horn that became dominant. However, before we launch into the Beasts of Revelation there is a point of clarification that probably needs to be made. Like Daniel, John writes about four beasts, which are not all exactly the same beast.

The Four Beasts of Revelation

There are several details about these prophecies about the Beast that must not be overlooked to get the accurate interpretation. First, we actually have four beasts in Revelation. The greater beast, which is also referred to as "*the great red dragon*," is a beast that has seven heads and ten horns:

> "*³Then another sign appeared in heaven: and behold, a **great red dragon** having **seven heads and ten horn**s, and on his heads were **seven diadems**." (Revelation 12:3)*

From this 12ᵗʰ chapter of Revelation we learn that the symbology of the Dragon introduces a supernatural element that involves Satan - "the Devil." * So this Dragon is identified with both the human element of earthly kingdoms with earthly rulers, and the Satanic element. The indication is that this beast is actually empowered by no less than Satan himself.

> *⁷And there was war in heaven, Michael and his angels waging war with the dragon. The dragon and his angels waged war, ⁸and they were not strong enough, and there was no longer a place found for them in heaven. ⁹And the **great dragon** was thrown down, **the serpent of old who is called the devil and Satan**, who deceives the whole world; he was thrown down to the earth, and his angels were thrown down with him." (Revelation 12:7-9)*

This scarlet Dragon, which has seven heads and ten horns, is called "a beast."

> "*¹And the **dragon** stood on the sand of the seashore. Then I saw a beast coming up out of the sea, having **ten horns and seven heads, and on his horns were ten diadems**, and on his heads were blasphemous names.." (Revelation 13:1)*

*[As people see the atrocities and unimaginable horrors that men inflict upon other men they often ask, how can human beings be so inhuman, so

evil, so cruel, so wicked? People are asking that today as they witness the incredibly evil atrocities being committed almost daily by Islamic religious extremists, the "terrorists." The Bible answers this question, though people may not like the answer, and many feel they are far to intelligent to believe in a cosmic arch-enemy in the spirit realm, which we call Satan - in fact many of them deny the existence of a spirit realm altogether. The question is, do they have better answers which really make more sense? To them maybe so, to many thinking people, not so much.]

Then we have another beast mentioned which is the seventh head of that "red Dragon" (also call *the scarlet beast* in 17:3). It is this beast, the seventh head of the Red Dragon, which has the ten horns.

"Here is the mind which has wisdom. The seven heads are seven mountains on which the woman sits, [10]and they are seven kings; five have fallen, one is, the other has not yet come; and when he comes, he must remain a little while. [11]The beast which was and is not, is himself also an eighth and is one of the seven, and he goes to destruction. [12]The ten horns which you saw are ten kings who have not yet received a kingdom, but they receive authority as kings with the beast for one hour." (Revelation 17:9-12)

Here we have the use of another metaphor, *"seven mountains,"* to interpret the symbolic *"heads"* metaphor, which is also interpreted for us as seven Kings, or kingdoms. We are told that all but the last one, the seventh, has already come and gone by now, the sixth being that which was extant at the time the prophecy was written. We know that was the Roman Empire. But that seventh king or kingdom, the seventh head or mountain, was still to come.

So then there is another beast, referred to as *"an eighth,"* which is the final form of that seventh head, the beast with the ten horns. That is the one that features one of the ten horns emerging as the dominant one, the global ruler we usually refer to as the Antichrist.These are the ones described in Revelation chapter thirteen and seventeen:

"Then I saw a beast coming up out of the sea, having ten horns and seven heads, and on his horns were ten diadems, and on his heads were blasphemous names.[2]And the beast which I saw was like a leopard, and his feet were like those

*of a bear, and his mouth like the mouth of a lion. And the dragon gave him his power and his throne and great authority. ³I saw **one of his head**s as if it had been slain, and his fatal wound was healed. And the whole earth was amazed and followed after **the beast**; ⁴they worshiped the dragon because he gave his authority to **the beast**; and they worshiped **the beast**, saying, 'Who is like **the beast**, and who is able to wage war with him?'" (Revelation 13:2-4)*

*"¹¹"**The beast** which was and is not, is himself **also an eighth** and is one of the seven, and he goes to destruction." (Revelation 17:11)*

Thus, in the seventeenth chapter (17:9-12 cited above) we see that the seventh head of the Dragon, is also the one with the ten horns. From 13:3 and 17:11 (cited above) we see that one of those ten horns emerges as the world leader, which much of the rest of that chapter goes on to describe. This world leader is then referred to as an *"eighth beast"* (17:11), which John refers to as a beast in the thirteenth chapter as well. Thus the form of that beast which involves the ten horns, a coalition of ten contemporary kings, is at least implicitly called a beast. And then the one who ascends to power over those other ten kings to become the world ruler which we now refer to as "the Antichrist," is also called a beast, the "eighth."

Then in the thirteenth chapter John describes yet another "beast," which he later refers to as "**the false prophet**" of that eighth beast. There, distinguishing it from what he calls "the first beast," which he has described in the first half of that chapter, he describes this second beast as follows:

"¹¹Then I saw another beast coming up out of the earth; and he had two horns like a lamb and he spoke as a dragon. ¹²He exercises all the authority of the first beast in his presence. And he makes the earth and those who dwell in it to worship the first beast, whose fatal wound was healed." (Revelation 13:11-12)

We see this second beast also referred to in the 19th chapter as "*the false prophet*":

"²⁰And the beast was seized, and with him the false prophet who performed the signs in his presence, by which he

deceived those who had received the mark of the beast and those who worshiped his image; these two were thrown alive into the lake of fire which burns with brimstone." (Revelation 19:20)

Thus to sum it up, there is the greater beast called the Great Red (Scarlet) Dragon. This beast has the seven heads. Then there is the seventh head of that greater Dragon, which consists of ten-horns, or a coalition of ten nations, which is also called a beast. Then one of those ten horns emerges to become the dominant leader of the ten (which becomes seven because he eliminates three when he takes over), and he is called "the eight" beast, and is known as "the Antichrist." And finally, the fourth is the "false prophet" of that eighth beast, the prophet of the Antichrist.

The Seven Heads of the Scarlet Beast

Now through the centuries Bible scholars have come up with all kinds of interpretations of this seven-headed beast of Revelation. For example, in more recent times men (conservative, evangelical, protestants who are literalists and futurists) have widely believed that the seven heads represented the seven hills of Rome, and that the Beast was the Catholic church (the Vatican being associated with Rome Italy) and the Antichrist would be a future Pope.* And indeed John does interpret the seven heads as seven mountains, and some historians have referred to Rome as the city on seven hills - although in fact there are more than seven hills and one is hard-pressed to identify which of all the hills would be included in the seven. There are many problems with these views, first scripturally speaking, and second with respect to current global developments.

*[There were variations of this interpretation, some saying the Catholic Church would be the Harlot Babylon which we find in Revelation seventeen, as the religious power which rides the Beast, until it is devoured by the Beast, but most believed the Antichrist would be a Pope.]

However, the simple truth is that John doesn't really leave much room for speculation and guess work on some of the key issues, as he tells us exactly what he meant by those symbols, and much more:

> *"and I saw a woman sitting on a scarlet beast, full of blasphemous names, having* **seven heads and ten horns***… When I saw her, I wondered greatly. [7]And the angel said to me, 'Why do you wonder? I will tell you the mystery of the woman and of the beast that carries her, which has the* **seven heads and the ten horns***.*
> *[8]The beast that you saw was, and is not, and is about to come up out of the abyss and go to destruction. And those who dwell on the earth, whose name has not been written in the book of life from the foundation of the world, will wonder when they see the beast, that* **he was and is not and will come***. [9]Here is the mind which has wisdom. The* **seven heads are seven mountains on which the woman sits, [10]and they are seven kings; five have fallen, one is, the other has not yet come; and when he comes, he must remain a little while. [11]The beast which was and is not, is himself also <u>an eighth and is one of the seven</u>, and he goes to destruction. [12]The ten horns which you saw are ten kings who have not yet received a kingdom, but they receive authority as kings with the beast for one hour.** *[13]These have one purpose, and they give their power and authority to the beast. [14]These will wage war against the Lamb, and the Lamb will overcome them, because He is Lord of lords and King of kings, and those who are with Him are the called and chosen and faithful.'"*
> *(Revelation 17:3-14)*

So, the brilliance and creativity of so many Bible scholars notwithstanding, in fact John pretty much just tells us what he means. **The seven heads are seven successive empires, five of which had come and passed from the scene as dominant world powers by the time John was writing this prophecy. The sixth he mentions as being in power as he was writing it. But the seventh he tells us is one that had not come yet, and when it comes it would not last long.** Then he goes on to tell us about another beast which he calls "*an eighth*," but also tells us that this eighth is, literally, "*of the seven*" (the word "*one*" as in "*one of the seven*" is not actually in the Greek text -

it was supplied by the translators). Thus we have five historic empires, which most scholars identify as Egypt, Assyria, Babylon, Medo-Persia, and the Alexandrian (Grecian) Empire* which "*have fallen.*" Of course we know that it was the Roman Empire that was dominant in John's day, so we know that was the sixth. Then John tells us that the seventh had not yet come. This would seem to rule out the Roman Empire as the one God had in mind as the seventh and eighth beasts when He inspired John to write this.

*[There is considerable room for debate as to exactly which historic empires should be included in these five. Egypt is particularly questionable as she never conquered or ruled over the Assyrian or the Babylonian empires - the Mesopotamian area. The original Babylonian empire of Hammurabi was conquered and ruled by the Assyrians until Nabopolassar re-established the supremacy of the Chaldean Empire, which became the Babylonian empire of Nebuchadnezzar II. However, exactly which empires were intended may not be all that relevant. It seems most likely that John was writing about at least the three that Daniel wrote about, Babylon, Medo-Persia, and Greece.]

By this point, having identified at least four of the five former empires (Egypt is debatable as to whether it belongs in this list) it should be obvious that at least in terms of today's world, and probably any time in the foreseeable future, the Bible is talking about the Islamic world. The Assyrian, Babylonian, Medo-Persian, and Greek Empires are all centered around what is known as Mesopotamia. The only thing all those countries in this general Mesopotamian region have in common today aside from their geography and history, is their religion - **Islam**.

The Ten Horns

Both Daniel and John go on to predict that the last empire, or "kingdom," will consist of ten "kings" or nations. John describes it as follows:

> "*12The ten horns which you saw are ten kings who have not yet received a kingdom, but they receive authority as kings with the beast for one hour. 13These have one purpose, and they give their power and authority to the beast.*"
> *(Revelation 17:12-13)*

John makes it crystal clear that the ten horns are ten contemporary kings that make up this seventh beast. Daniel also makes this rather clear in his predictions, beginning with the image of chapter two with two feet and ten toes, and the fourth beast of chapter seven, which also had ten horns:

*[33]its legs of iron, **its feet** partly of iron and partly of clay. ... [41]In that you saw **the feet and toes**, partly of potter's clay and partly of iron, it will be a divided kingdom; but it will have in it the toughness of iron, inasmuch as you saw the iron mixed with common clay. (Daniel 2:33 & 41)*

*"[7]After this I kept looking in the night visions, and behold ,a fourth beast, dreadful and terrifying and extremely strong; and it had large iron teeth. It devoured and crushed and trampled down the remainder with its feet; and it was different from all the beasts that were before it, and **it had ten horns**." (Daniel 7:7)*

"[24]As for the ten horns, out of this kingdom ten kings will arise;..." (Daniel 7:24a)

At the present time perhaps the most popular interpretation for the last fifty plus years has been what is called "the Revived Roman Empire" theory. Rather than just seeing the Catholic Church as the Beast, or the Harlot, and the Pope as the Antichrist, the so-called revived Roman Empire is then interpreted as being the European Union (EU), or European Common Market (ECM). The Antichrist would be the leader or president of that coalition of European nations. Some even combine the two, with both the EU and the Roman Catholic Church as major players, a few still seeing the Antichrist as a Pope and head of the EU. Ironically some see this Antichrist as a Jew - which would hardly be Roman. However, aside from the many problems scripturally and logically with those theories, such interpretations require a shift in focus from what Daniel so clearly prophesied. With respect to the geographical areas involved and the cultures and people groups, the focus of Daniel's prophecies were clearly the middle-eastern, Mesopotamian area. The European Union as a revived Roman Empire shifts that focus dramatically from a Mesopotamian focus to a European one, which is ostensibly Christian (albeit in name only). Of course we all know how those Christian Europeans hate the Jews, hate Christians, and tend to behead their enemies - right?

Understandably when the EU was made up of ten nations, some jumped to the conclusion that it was the ten-horned beast - men tend to do that with prophecy (that was also an era when many if not most prophecy buffs and preachers were sure Christ would be coming back within the next decade or so). Today, with a membership of 28 nations (probably more by the time this is published - though possibly less as some default on their debts and others withdraw from the Union), there is precious little correlation between the EU, and Daniel's and John's prophecies with respect to the ten horns of the Beast. Clearly the focus of Daniel's three beasts of the fourth chapter (the lion, the bear, and the leopard) is the Mesopotamia area and cultures, i.e. the Middle-East - not Europe. You can pick any ten nations in that Mesopotamian area, and you have Islamists dominated and controlled cultures and governments. You still have Assyrians, Syrians, Medes (some scholars believe that the modern day descendants of the Medes are the Kurds, though this is debated by others), Persians, Arabs, and if you include the southern neighbor, Egyptians. So that coalition of ten of those nations will be a conglomeration of all those ancient people groups and their original lands. Only then do the prophecies of Daniel cited below, make sense, that when Christ comes back He will actually destroy all those previous empires at the same time as they will all be part of that end-time ten-horned beast: *

> *35 "Then the iron, the clay, the bronze, the silver and the gold were crushed **all at the same time** and became like chaff from the summer threshing floors; and the wind carried them away so that not a trace of them was found. ..." (Daniel 2:35)*

> *"45Inasmuch as you saw that a stone was cut out of the mountain without hands and that it crushed the iron, the bronze, the clay, the silver and the gold...," (Daniel 2:45)*

*[It is telling that so many Bible scholars who are claiming to be literalists seem to miss or ignore such important details - how can a European Union

Beast and European president be a fulfillment of these prophecies such that when Christ destroys them He will also be destroying those preceding Babylonian, Medo-Persian, and Alexandrian Empires? To say that it is true because He destroys the whole earth is to render such details meaningless as predictors.]

It may be taking the symbology too far, but we see from Daniel's prophecy featuring the image of the man, that the final kingdom is represented by two feet and ten toes. Today's Islamic world is very divided, but mostly into two camps - Sunnis and Shia. It seems unlikely that an empire will emerge like the previous empires, with one king who conquers them militarily and they all become one big empire. Daniel describes it as follows:

> *"42As the toes of the feet were partly of iron and partly of pottery, so some of the kingdom will be strong and part of it will be brittle. 43And in that you saw the iron mixed with common clay, they will combine with one another in the seed of men; but they will not adhere to one another, even as iron does not combine with pottery." (Daniel 2:42-43)*

However, like the feet of that image Nebuchadnezzar saw and Daniel interpreted, it does seem not only believable but almost likely that at least ten of those Islamic nations will be able to come together into a cooperative coalition, and pick one leader to preside over their coalition.

Now it may come as a shock to some, but the Islamic nations in the former "cradle of civilization" area, the Middle-East, is prophesied in the Bible as becoming the main attraction on the stage of global conflict. It's not Europe, or Russia, or China, or Bosnia, nor Japan, nor North or South Korea, nor South America nor North America, not even India or Pakistan.

Does this ring a bell or sound at all believable? Iraq, Iran, Syria - the focus of world attention and intense conflict? Islam, the "peaceful religion," threatening not only the peace and even existence of every one in the region, but of the rest of the world as well, including the western world? Who could ever believe that? Just a bunch of religious fanatics, Bible thumpers, those fanatical extremist right-wing Christians take all that Bible prophecy stuff serious, - right? Or, maybe not! Anybody checked in on world news recently - like in the last twenty or more years? Does 911 call anything to mind? Ever heard of the Arab Spring? How about routine bombings, mass killings and beheadings? Do the names Al Qaeda or ISIS mean anything to anyone? Where is all this happening on a daily basis?

The Lion, Bear, Leopard, Ten-horned Beast and The "Little Horn"

About this ten-horned beast John writes:
*²And the beast which I saw was like a **leopard**, and his feet were like those of a **bear**, and his mouth like the mouth of a **lion**." (Revelation 13:2)*

When we realize that the symbology of the lion, bear and leopard as already appearing in Daniel's prophecy is now applied to describe the ten horned beast in Johns prophecy, it seems to give us another important clue as to the identity of this beast. Daniel interprets for us what these symbols represent - the lion being the Babylonian empire, the bear being the Medo-Persian Empire, and the leopard being the Greek or Alexandrian Empire. Applying this information to John's description of this end-time seven-headed ten-horned beast we are not really being speculative in understanding that some form of the earlier Babylonian, Medo-Persian and Alexandrian Empires will be part of the makeup of this final beast - Daniel's fourth beast of Daniel 7, and John's seventh and eighth beast of Revelation 13 and 17. In fact it would seem that the implication is that the main body of the beast will be that Grecian element (now Syrian), with the mouth-piece being the Babylonian element (now Arabic and Iraqi), and the feet that does the trampling over those he conquers being the Medo-Persian element (now mostly Persian or Iranian).

Translating this into today's world, the leopard would seem to be mostly the Syrian element - the descendants of Seleucid (in the line of Antiochus IV Epiphanes), which are mostly in power in the area of modern Syria. This would also include that people group which was formerly Assyrian. Then we have the feet with which the Beast tramples its enemies, which is the bear, the Persian element, which is now mostly Iran. According to Daniel it is the feet of this beast which tramples down all of its enemies (Daniel 7:7 & 19). Iran may actually be the most militant and militarily powerful element of this beast - which certainly matches up to the way the situation in the Middle-East is developing at the time of this writing. Iran is aggressively involved around the world, especially in the Islamic world, and Iran is developing into a nuclear power, with no one able or willing to stop her.

Then we see this Babylonian element, which John tells us is the mouth of this beast. Babylon in today's world is associated with Iraq, the city of Babylon of course being in Iraq. It is interesting that Daniel's "little horn," which becomes the dominant leader of the ten-horned coalition, which John then refers to as an eighth beast, is described by both Daniel and John as having a big blasphemous mouth:

*"⁸While I was contemplating the horns, behold, another horn, a little one, came up among them, and three of the first horns were pulled out by the roots before it; and behold, **this horn possessed eyes like the eyes of a man and a mouth uttering great boasts**". (Daniel 7:7-8)*
*"¹¹Then I kept looking because of the **sound of the boastful words which the horn was speaking;**" (Daniel 7:11)*
*"²⁰ᵇ ...that horn which had eyes and **a mouth uttering great boasts** and which was larger in appearance than its associates." (Daniel 7:20b)*
*"²⁴As for the ten horns, out of this kingdom ten kings will arise; and another will arise after them, and he will be different from the previous ones and will subdue three kings. ²⁵**He will speak out against the Most High** and wear down the saints of the Highest One, and he will intend to make alterations in times and in law; and they will be given into his hand for a time, times, and half a time." (Daniel 7:24-25)*

*"⁵There was given to him **a mouth speaking arrogant words and blasphemies**, and authority to act for forty-two months was given to him. ⁶And **he opened his mouth in***

blasphemies against God, to blaspheme His name and His tabernacle, that is, those who dwell in heaven." (Revelation 13:5-6)

In recent times we have seen rulers of Islamic countries which seem to fit this description, such as Sadaam Hussein in Iraq, and President Ahmadinejad in Iran, who were very boisterous and blasphemous. The present Ayatollah in Iran is similarly noted for his pronouncements and proclamations of such a nature, as are countless other Imam's and Islamic clerics and leaders. It is probably to be expected that such will be the case with whoever emerges as the ultimate leader of the Islamic world. The implication of these prophecies by Daniel and John would seem to be that this leader with the big mouth will be associated with Babylon, which would involve Iraq. However, in light of what is going on in Iraq today, it is not at all clear that this leader will necessarily be Iraqi as it is so divided that **this leader may actually be Syrian backed by Iranian power, but will make Babylon his capitol city, his home base of operations**. Even Sadaam was Iraqi, but became the head of the Ba'athist Party, which was originally Syrian (the party of the ruling al-Assad family still in power there as of this writing). But like Sadaam Hussein tried to do, he may try to present himself as a resurrected or reincarnated Nebuchadnezzar (or Hammurabi) reviving the Babylonian Empire to its glory days as the first great world empire.

It seems that what we can glean from this as a minimum is the prediction that at least **Syria, and Iran and Iraq will be part of this coalition of ten mid-eastern nations**, which will make up the seventh beast of Revelation. It is also pretty clear that their leader, the one we call the Antichrist, will come from one of these three major players. Putting all the pieces together it seems possible if not likely that **he will come from the Seleucid line**, like Antiochus IV Epiphanes, which would be more Syrian than Persian or Arabic. However, as we will see from John's predictions in Revelation, he will make **his capital and home base, Babylon** in Iraq (the mouth of the lion). But his **military power will probably be the Iranian** element (the

70

feet of the bear) - which makes sense now as we see Iran
becoming a nuclear power, as well as quite well armed with
conventional weaponry.
[Iran has an active military of over ½ million men, with another 1.8
million active reserve, with an impressive array of missiles, tanks,
armored vehicles, artillery, aircraft and ships. She is backed by Russia
who supplies her with arms.]

The Assyrian Connection

However, this eighth beast may also be of Assyrian
descent, as the former Assyria became the Syrian or Seleucid
kingdom, and the people and culture and land of Assyria were
absorbed into that Seleucid Kingdom. Today's Assyrians are
divided between those who are still there, and the "diaspora" -
those which have left their homeland, mostly to escape
persecution. Most of the ethnic Assyrians left in the homeland
now live in Northern Iraq (some sources say about 1.5 or 1.2
million, others say only 300,000 since Sadaam) and Syria
(about 0.7 million), with communities spread around the
middle-east (From "Brief History of Assyria,"
www.aina.org/brief.html.). One source gives the following
information:

"What we now know as Syria once consisted of several
city-states, which were later incorporated into the Assyrian
Empire. The region became known as 'Abar-Nahra ('Across
the River') by the Assyrians, Babylonians and later by the
Persians. The Greeks and the Romans knew it as Syria,
short for Assyria, because it had long remained under
Assyrian rule ... When, in 64 BC the Roman Emperor
Pompey annexed the land west of Euphrates and
incorporated them into the Roman Empire, the area came to
be known as Syria, short for Assyria, as Assyria proper lay
within the boundaries of the Persian Empire…. As The
Encyclopedia Americana writes, under the entry Syria, 'It is
now certain that the name "Syria" is derived from the older
"Assyria."'" (from "Who Are The Assyrians?" Nicholas Aljeloo,
The Assyrian Australian Academic Society (TAAAS), Sydney,
Australia, July 2, 2000. ag@ninevah.com
(www.nineveh.com/whoarewe.htm))

[While this has been debated by scholars, there is now pretty good evidence (in the form of the Çineköy inscription") that the name "Syria" is derived from "Assyria." It seems that "Syria" is a Greek corruption of "Assyria."]

So why is all this interesting or relevant, about Assyria? The answer is, because we have several prophecies in other Old Testament passages which seem to be about this end-times ruler, and he is referred to as an Assyrian:

> "5   *This One will be our peace.*
> *When the **Assyrian** invades our land,*
> *When he tramples on our citadels,*
> *Then we will raise against him*
> *Seven shepherds and eight leaders of men.*
> 6   *They will shepherd the land of Assyria with the sword,*
> *The land of Nimrod at its entrances;*
> *And He will deliver us from the **Assyrian***
> *When he attacks our land*
> *And when he tramples our territory." (Micah 5:5-6)*

> "26*The light of the moon will be as the light of the sun, and the light of the sun will be seven times brighter, like the light of seven days, on the day the Lord binds up the fracture of His people and heals the bruise He has inflicted...*
> 30   *And the Lord will cause His voice of authority to be heard,*
> *And the descending of His arm to be seen in fierce anger,*
> *And in the flame of a consuming fire*
> *In cloudburst, downpour and hailstones.*
> 31   *For at the voice of the Lord **Assyria** will be terrified,*
> *When He strikes with the rod.*
> 32   *And every blow of the rod of punishment,*
> *Which the Lord will lay on him,*
> *Will be with the music of tambourines and lyres;*
> *And in battles, brandishing weapons, He will fight them."*
> *(Isaiah 30:26-32)*

Then we have other passages, which appear to be among the dual prophecies discussed earlier, such as Isaiah 10:12, and 14:22-26. Interestingly the passage in the 14th chapter of Isaiah is mostly dealing with Babylon as the target of God's judgment, and seemingly without changing the subject refers to it as Assyria:

> *"²²'I will rise up against them,' declares the Lord of hosts, 'and will cut off from **Babylon** name and survivors, offspring and posterity,' declares the Lord. ²³'I will also make it a possession for the hedgehog and swamps of water, and I will sweep it with the broom of destruction,' declares the Lord of hosts. ²⁴The Lord of hosts has sworn saying, 'Surely, just as I have intended so it has happened, and just as I have planned so it will stand, ²⁵to break **Assyria** in My land, and I will trample him on My mountains. Then his yoke will be removed from them and his burden removed from their shoulder. ²⁶This is the plan devised against the whole earth; and this is the hand that is stretched out against all the nations.'" (Isaiah 14:22-26)*

If I am understanding this correctly, the implication would seem to be that there is some identity between the two, Babylon and Assyria, in this end-times beast. In fact, the ruler who will be the Antichrist could be of Syrian and Assyrian origin, but also be the Babylonian ruler, with his capital in the city of Babylon, in Iraq.

Now if we are strictly literal in insisting upon an ethnic Assyrian - not just taken in the sense of Syrian - that is to be the Antichrist, and also a Muslim, then we may have a problem since today's true Assyrians are reportedly mostly Christian in their religion. However, since there is this name identity, such that what once was called Assyrian is now called Syrian, it is not necessary to insist upon the Antichrist as being an ethnic Syrian for the prophecies to be accurate. Furthermore, the connection to Syria is the fact that he will come from the Seleucid line of kings, which reigned over the lands and peoples who were descended from the ancient Assyrians. Hence when the Bible prophets spoke about an Assyrian, in today's world it is Syrian because the name has changed, as discussed above.

However, if indeed this Islamic Antichrist were to be an ethnic Assyrian, that could be in fulfillment of a specific detail of Daniel's prophecy discussed above, when he predicts that this king of the North would *"show no regard for the gods of his fathers"* (Daniel 11:37). Since Assyrians as a people group are known to be Christians, for him to present himself to the world as a Muslim would certainly be abandoning the faith of his fathers, showing no regard for the god of his fathers. If such a person should emerge as a leader of an Islamic coalition, it would certainly be an impressive fulfillment of such a detailed prophecy, leaving little doubt about his identity as the biblical Antichrist. But again, such need not be the case for a Syrian ruler who also becomes the Babylonian ruler, to fulfill even the prophecies referring to him as an Assyrian, since that is the ancient Hebrew name for what now is included under the name Syrian.

The Crowns (Diadems)
One of the points being made in this book is that these predictions in the Bible are not the kind other famed secular prophets made, which were short on specifics by which the predictions could be tested with any rational degree of confidence in their accuracy. And even with all the specific details we see how men can find many very different interpretations of them - until they actually occur. Even then in some cases men don't recognize the fulfillment when they do occur, usually because of their presuppositions - mistaken presuppositions. A good example of this are the Preterits of our day who fail to see the rebirth of Israel as a nation, and the developments in the Middle-East as fulfilling prophecy at all, because they are committed to the view that it was virtually all fulfilled by AD 70 when Rome destroyed Jerusalem. Of course to maintain that view they have to accept a method of interpretation which is anything but literal, except for those parts which in fact actually have been fulfilled - the rise and fall of those ancient empires - that they sometimes take pretty literally. However, if we choose not to take prophecy as literally as the language allows, then the specifics don't mean a whole lot, and we might as well be dealing with a Nostradamus or an Edgar Cayce.

For those of us who do take the literal approach, it is

essential to pay attention to the specifics. Reality is quite specific when it happens. That an empire or a king, or a government, or a culture or a movement of some kind is going to eventually pass from the scene, that is a given in most cases. To predict such a thing does not require divine revelation. In fact men can often predict trends in general terms with a high degree of accuracy. But to predict exact specifics about how even such predictable trends will actually transpire, that is beyond the natural realm of human capability or even statistical probability.

We saw in the previous chapter how Daniel predicted not only the big picture about the empires that would rise and fall, but gave amazing detail about how and even in some cases when significant events and developments would happen. A fool may pass them off as coincidence, or try to come up with a natural explanation, but their attempts to do so reveal what they are - fools (God's word for them, not mine). As the saying goes, "the devil is in the details" (whatever that means), which applies in this case for those who ignorantly overlook, or choose to ignore the details. Any interpretations or applications such as scenarios of end-times developments in the world, that miss or misinterpret the details, is destined for the ash-heap of so many failures to get it right that it would be almost impossible to address them all. On the other hand, it is just such detail that should cause the rational person to conclude that such predictions must be coming from a higher power (just maybe the one that those prophecies themselves claim to be the source).

So what we see in these prophecies in Revelation is a small detail, and would appear to be a discrepancy, a contradiction:

*"³Then another sign appeared in heaven: and behold, a great red dragon having seven heads and ten horns, and on his heads were **seven diadems**." (Revelation 12:3 emphasis added)*

*"¹And the dragon stood on the sand of the seashore. Then I saw a beast coming up out of the sea, having ten horns and seven heads, and on his horns were **ten diadems,**…"*

(Revelation 13:1 emphasis added)

Is it seven diadems, or is it ten? Ok, the skeptics have us now - see the Bible is full of contradictions - right? Well that could be, but like so many imagined contradictions maybe the reader is missing something. What if we let scripture interpret it for us? This is why we need Daniel to interpret Revelation, and Revelation to understand what Daniel prophesied about the end-times. We have seen that both of these references are describing the end-times beast and the other passages explain for us what the heads are and what the horns represent. However, John does not go into explaining the "diadems," or "crowns" - perhaps because it is pretty obvious what would be meant by a crown. The "diadem" or crown is always a symbol of a ruler or sovereign of some kind. In our day such would be probably called a sovereign nation or a ruler of such a nation. We have seen already that the horns represent rulers which he calls "kings" - John tells us this in Revelation 17:12. But the global scene that he is describing is not a static picture, as in a snapshot. Rather it is more like a video, which he saw in a vision, a "moving picture," in which much was happening. Scenes were coming and going, and the global situation being portrayed was in a state of continuous and rapid change. This change involved this ten-horned beast as well as everything else. Daniel fills in some of the detail with respect to the evolution of this beast:

*"⁷"After this I kept looking in the night visions, and behold, a fourth beast, dreadful and terrifying and extremely strong; and it had large iron teeth. It devoured and crushed and trampled down the remainder with its feet; and it was different from all the beasts that were before it, and **it had ten horns**. ⁸While I was contemplating the horns, behold, another horn, a little one, came up among them, **and three of the first horns were pulled out by the roots before it**; and behold, this horn possessed eyes like the eyes of a man and a mouth uttering great boasts." (Daniel 7:7-8 emphasis added)*

"²⁴'As for the ten horns, out of this kingdom ten kings will arise; and another will arise after them, and he will be

So we see that when this eighth beast (the Antichrist) emerges and comes to power it will be a coalition of ten nations, with ten crowns (sovereign states with their own rulers) which elect, or accept him as their coalition leader. However, once he succeeds in consolidating his power, he essentially deposes three of the government heads, the "horns" or "kings," probably because he perceives them to be a threat. If we look at trends today we see a rather big movement in the geo-political realm toward a realignment of the mid-eastern nations, redefining their borders. This is not something new as it was done in the 20th century, which gave Israel a homeland, carved out Lebanon and Jordan and remapped the whole region. Today the Kurds want and will fight for their own nation. Many think that Iraq must be divided into separate states to stop the constant infighting there. When a leader arises in that area, who can bring any degree of unity and semblance of peace (or the promise of peace) to the region, he will be embraced not only by the Islamic world, but possibly even by the whole world (speaking in very general terms of course). When his proposal for bringing such peace involves a realignment or reorganization of his coalition of ten Islamic countries, such that national borders are redefined, who will object or find it unacceptable - except those who become the deposed?

On the other hand, it might be that this powerful ruler, which literally the Bible says will become a world ruler (Daniel 7:23, Revelation 13:3, 7-8, 12, 14, 16-17), may just eliminate three of his coalition member states by military or political takeover. Daniel does tell us that this Antichrist will invade Egypt and Libya and Sudan (literally "Ethiopia" which we are being told is mostly today's Sudan) will follow (whatever that means) - perhaps they are the three that get uprooted, though it is debatable as to whether or not they would part of that initial coalition of ten. Nevertheless, when we see a ruler, or "President," who comes to power over a coalition of ten Islamic nations, but then in some way eliminates three of them such that they become seven entities - you might seriously consider believing that you are seeing the Antichrist both Daniel and John are describing.

The Woman the Harlot Babylon

Up to this point we have ignored a key piece of this puzzle, and that is the Harlot Babylon John writes about in Revelation. In fact, without Revelation we may not even recognize that element or aspect of this future empire of the Beast which the Harlot and Babylon represent. Daniel only predicted and described the Beast and that last leader or ruler, probably because the Beast and this Harlot were so enmeshed and entangled with each other that the distinctions between them are not so obvious and not essential to what Daniel was trying to communicate. John however is giving us some more specific details so that we can recognize that end-time system of government and the Antichrist, when they do appear. Thus he writes the following:

> "*¹Then one of the seven angels who had the seven bowls came and spoke with me, saying, 'Come here, I will show you the judgment of **the great harlot** who sits on many waters, ²with whom the kings of the earth committed acts of immorality, and those who dwell on the earth were made drunk with the wine of her immorality.' ³And he carried me away in the Spirit into a wilderness; and I saw a woman sitting on a scarlet beast, full of blasphemous names, having seven heads and ten horns. ⁴The woman was clothed in purple and scarlet, and adorned with gold and precious stones and pearls, having in her hand a gold cup full of abominations and of the unclean things of her immorality, ⁵and on her forehead a name was written, a mystery, 'BABYLON THE GREAT, THE MOTHER OF HARLOTS AND OF THE ABOMINATIONS OF THE EARTH.' ⁶And I saw the woman drunk with the blood of the saints, and with the blood of the witnesses of Jesus. When I saw her, I wondered greatly. ⁷And the angel said to me, 'Why do you wonder? I will tell you the mystery of the woman and of the beast that carries her, which has the*

seven heads and the ten horns.'" (Revelation 17:1-7)

*"[15]And he said to me, 'The waters which you saw where the harlot sits, are peoples and multitudes and nations and tongues. [16]And the ten horns which you saw, and the beast, these will hate the harlot and will make her desolate and naked, and will eat her flesh and will burn her up with fire. [17]For God has put it in their hearts to execute His purpose by having a common purpose, and by giving their kingdom to the beast, until the words of God will be fulfilled. [18]**The woman whom you saw is the great city**, which reigns over the kings of the earth.'" (Revelation 17:15-18)*

Having already identified the *"Scarlet Beast"* with the seven heads and ten horns, as we have in the preceding text, helps us in the task of identifying this Woman, the Harlot, Babylon the Great. We now know that this "woman" is not one of the seven empires or "kings." It is not the coalition of 10 which becomes 7 nations or "kings" which make up the 7th Beast. And it is not the final "king" or the eighth Beast, the Antichrist. This in itself eliminates a number of the many theories regarding both the various beasts, and the Antichrist, and Babylon, and this much we know simply from what John explicitly tells us here. So thus far we can have some pretty good ideas about who this woman Babylon is **not**. But figuring out who she is will take some careful examination of what John has given us as clues.

Here again we have some detail, which if missed or misinterpreted will cause us to get the wrong interpretation, the wrong picture, as many have already done. However, this is also the piece that takes the most discernment, and is not so clearly explained in scripture - we do have to dig to make sense of it. For that reason it would be grandiose to claim that I know for sure exactly what it all means, or that my interpretation is the final word. That being the case, I can't claim absolute certainty about much of the rest of the scenarios I will propose, with respect to anything affected by the interpretation of this imagery involving the symbolic Woman riding on the Beast, the

Harlot, Babylon the Great. However, we can put some things together and see if they are first consistent with everything scripture has to say about it, and secondly if they make sense.

We begin with what John tells us in Revelation. In our text in chapter seventeen we are given the following information about her:

a. She *"sits on many waters"* (17:1), which is explained in verse 15: *"The waters which you saw where the harlot sits, are peoples and multitudes and nations and tongues"* (17:15). Thus we know that **her realm of influence, and her power base, if you will, from which she draws her support, is an international, multiethnic *"multitude."*** This supports the notion that she represents a global, one-world system. This term *"many waters"* seems to refer more to the people, as opposed to the *"kings of the earth,"* or the ruler, or a system represented by the "beast." Thus, we see that this "woman" **seduces the multitudes as well as the world rulers, suggesting a world-wide popular following.**

b. She is in a relationship with *"the kings of the earth"* which is characterized as being immoral, such that her influence upon them is in some sense **intoxicating**, apparently contributing to their own immorality. The symbolic name, *"harlot,"* seems to imply that this is in some sense an adulterous relationship, which **would suggest a religious element involving idolatry.** In the following passages, (v. 6, and chapter 18) this intoxication or **drunkenness** is alluded to repeatedly, from which we gather that it **included persecution and martyrdom of the saints. It also included some form of immoral sensuality that is somehow connected with wealth, as in the material enrichment of those who become involved with her in this immoral relationship**. Repeatedly in the next chapter (Revelation 18) the economic connection is made between the wealth of the *"Merchants of the earth,"* and the shipping industry, and *"Babylon,"* (one of her names) which is also identified as the *"great city."* There we learn that she is also apparently **a center of world-wide trade and commerce**, at least in the marketing, or consumption of *"luxurious"* products (see 18:14). From this one gets the sense that the economic part of the *"immoral sensuality"* with which she *"deceives…all the nations of the earth"* (18:23), is the materialism associated with luxurious lifestyles. The immorality, or *"wine of the passion of her immorality"* (18:3) might also have some connection with **"*unclean spirits*"** or **"*demons*"** as mentioned in 18:2 (more on this in the following).

c. She is also in a relationship with the *"scarlet beast"* - the seven headed ten-horned beast, which is described and explained further in the last half of this chapter. There we see that this beast is actually representative of world rulers down through history and up to the final world ruler yet to come - the *"eighth beast"* (17:11). Just as she is sitting on the many waters, so she is seen by John, *"sitting on"* the scarlet beast. Her relationship with this beast, however, is a very clear indication that **she does not represent a person - as in "the antichrist" - nor a system that is only connected with a certain age** (such as the first century AD per the Preterists)**, or a particular culture** (such as the Jews). **She is a system that has been involved down through the ages. She has been involved with at least the *"five kings"* mentioned who have come and gone (17:10). She is still involved with the *"kings"* extant at the time John is writing this. And she will be involved with that *"king"* which was still to come, which will be one of the seven revived, and will become the eighth, which is usually identified with the Antichrist.** This would seem to be somewhat of a **symbiotic relationship between the woman and the beast** almost until the end.

d. There is a name written on her forehead, **"*Babylon the Great, the Mother of Harlots and Abominations of the Earth*."** This name is referred to as *"a mystery,"* but then this *"mystery"* is explained (in part at least) as well as the mystery of the beast that carries her, in the last half of this seventeenth chapter. While verses 8-14 (of Revelation 17) are mostly explaining the seven heads and ten horns of the beast, verse 15 returns to the subject of the woman, which is the main topic of the whole next chapter (Revelation 18) up to the third verse of chapter nineteen.

e. What we are specifically told in this chapter about *"the*

Woman," is that **the ten horns of the Beast will *"hate"* the woman** ("*the harlot*"), **and will *"make her desolate and naked, and will eat her flesh and will burn her up with fire"*** (17:16). In doing this they will be accomplishing God's purpose, to fulfill His word. In telling us this, God makes it clear that there is a distinction to be made between "*the Woman*" and "*the Scarlet Beast,*" such that this "*Harlot*" and the so-called "Antichrist" are not one and the same.

f. We are also told that this "*Woman*" is "***the great city which reigns over the kings of the earth***" (17:18). This rather clearly distinguishes it from Jerusalem which is also referred to as "*the great city*" in Revelation 11:8. But Jerusalem has not in any sense been a center of influential power and control over the kings of the earth (since the days of David and Solomon), especially the kings referred to as the seventh head of the beast. It would also seem to eliminate Rome, inasmuch as her great power and influence has been diminished to the point that no one could seriously contend that she still "*reigns over the kings of the earth.*" She certainly wasn't "the great city" which in any sense reigned over the kings of the earth in the days of the Babylonian, Medo-Persian and Alexandrian Empires. On the other hand, as we will see even more clearly in the following, a literal city does seem to be indicated here, with no real need to spiritualize this, or regard it is merely symbolic.

Although there is no city that has maintained a position of such prominence and dominance as a political world power over that whole period of history, perhaps what we should be looking for is **a city that is historically representative of the seat and center of origin of <u>the system</u>** which is being referred to here as "*the Woman.*" That system called "*the Woman,*" must be one that has in some sense reigned over the Kings of the earth, and will until the ten horns finally destroy her. Perhaps it would also be worth considering, and certainly less speculative than other options being proposed, that the city we are looking for is exactly what we are being told it is in this passage - none other than that ancient city of "***Babylon.***" That is the city and empire where Daniel's prophecies begin, the first of the seven kingdoms of Daniel chapter 2, and the first of the four kingdoms of Daniel 7.

The Metaphor of the Harlot

Taking a closer look at some of these, the first thing we might consider is how this metaphor of "harlotry" is normally used in the Bible, when it is referring to nations, or people groups as opposed to individuals. God often referred to Israel's unfaithfulness to Him as "whoring," "adultery," playing the harlot, when they apostatized spiritually and began to worship other gods and idols:

*"16The Lord said to Moses, 'Behold, you are about to lie down with your fathers; and this people will arise and **play the harlot with the strange gods of the land**, into the midst of which they are going, and will forsake Me and break My covenant which I have made with them.'" (Deuteronomy 31:16,* see also Ezekiel 16 for example).

This is not to say that it only referred to idolatry, because it also involved their entanglement with the heathen nations around them in other ways. They not only became corrupted by the religious aspects of those other cultures, but their immoral lifestyles as well. So when we see the Bible using the metaphor of "harlotry" or "adultery" we know that it is referring to a spiritual condition of being unfaithful to God, turning to other "gods" whatever they may be. Thus **when we see this symbol of the harlot, as associated with this end-time beast, it seems to be representative of the spiritual and religious element of this last empire, as well as its predecessors (the seven heads of the Dragon).**

Perhaps for this reason many in the past have interpreted this Harlot Babylon as either Jerusalem and apostate Israel, or Rome and apostate Christendom, as in the Roman Catholic Church. This latter popular interpretation of Babylon as being Rome, hence apostate Christendom with the Pope as the Antichrist, was popularized by C.I. Scofield in the notes in his Scofield Reference Bible which became the most popular Bible among evangelical Protestants for much of the 20th century. Scofield describes this Babylon as involving "ecclesiastical Babylon" and "a political Babylon." He says it is the latter which is "the beast's confederate empire." However, scripture doesn't say that the Harlot Babylon is riding the Beast Babylon, and we will see that the fall of "Babylon" precedes the fall of the Beast and the Antichrist. In fact, it is that beast which ultimately attacks and devours the Harlot, and the whole 18th chapter of Revelation is about how that affects all the rest of the earth - which of course has to happen some period of time before the Beast itself is destroyed along with the whole earth. Nonetheless, other than changing Babylon to Rome and ignoring the distinctions made between them, Scofield may not be too far off in seeing an ecclesiastical versus a political element in this empire of the Beast. The big difference is that **it is the Beast that represents the political and military element, while the Harlot Babylon is the ecclesiastical or religious element** (though there is little to support the theory that Babylon is really either Jerusalem, or Rome).

It is clear that the apostatized Christian Church may be a part of this metaphorical *"Great Harlot,"* at least in the sense that it will go along with and not resist her. She may even become deceived by the *"Beast,"* and the *"Prophet of the Beast."* However this alone is hardly an adequate fulfillment of the symbology or the descriptions we see here in Revelation seventeen and eighteen. First, in no sense has the Christian Church been sitting on or riding the *"Beast"* over the period of time that said *"Beast"* has existed in the form of at least six different *"kings,"* up to the present. Only the era and empire of Constantine would resemble this metaphorical relationship of the Woman riding the Beast, with Christianity of any form being the Woman. But there are still at least five other empires that must be accounted for according to John's revelation.

Second, the apostatized Christian Church has had little to do historically speaking with the nations and cultures and ethnic groups of the Mesopotamian area, which for many reasons as discussed above is identifiable with this *"Scarlet Beast."* Nor is there any reason to speculate that some version of Christianity will somehow come to dominate the Islamic world of today. That would be necessary to have the apostatized Christian Church become the *"Great Harlot,"* which is also identified with "*Babylon the Great*," which is in turn identified with "*the Great City Babylon*." It is clear that in no sense could it be said that the Christian Church in any form, apostate or otherwise, is reigning over the kings of the earth today. Nor are the merchants of the earth being significantly enrichened by said apostate Christian Church.

It is understandable how the Roman Catholic Church could have been perceived as playing that role back in the era of King Constantine and the Crusaders, or perhaps during the "dark ages." But she is no longer a **dominant** power in the world today, as she once was. Certainly it would be difficult to make any connection between Roman Catholicism, or any form of apostate Christianity, and either the historic or modern day Babylon, other than some of the Pagan influences that have found their way into the religious observances of the church. But such would be almost the reverse of what is described here in Revelation, where the "*Harlot*" is said to be controlling the global political situation, not just infiltrated by it as the Catholic Church and apostate Christianity have been.

We do have some clues provided in our text however, as to what the spiritual immorality and adultery may include. Once again we have clear correspondence between what John writes in Revelation about this "*Babylon the Great*" in chapter eighteen, and what was prophesied by an Old Testament prophet:

*"...for she says in her heart, '**I sit as a queen** and I am **not a widow**, and will never see mourning.' For this reason in one day her plagues will come, pestilence and mourning and famine, and she will be **burned up with fire**; for the Lord God who judges her is strong."* (Revelation 18:7-8)

*"Come down and sit in the dust, O virgin daughter of **Babylon** ... for you will no longer be called the **queen** of kingdoms ... you said, '**I shall be a queen forever**.' Now then, hear this, you sensual one, who dwells securely, who says in your heart, 'I am, and there is no one besides me, **I shall not sit as a widow**, nor shall I know loss of children. They shall come on you in full measure in spite of your*

***many sorceries**, in spite of the great power of your spells. ... evil will come on you which you will not know how to charm away; and **disaster** will fall on you for which you cannot atone, and **destruction** about which you do not know will come on you suddenly... [14]Behold, they have become like stubble, **fire burns them; they cannot deliver themselves from the power of the flame**;... [15] So have those become to you with whom you have labored, who have trafficked with you from your youth;"* (Isaiah 47:1-11&14-15a)

We see that the judgment mentioned by Isaiah is described in terms of *"**fire**"* which clearly corresponds again with the judgment mentioned above by John, *"she will be burned up with fire."* Furthermore, Isaiah goes on to define this destruction further as coming at the hands of *"**those ... with whom you have labored, who have <u>trafficked</u> with you from your youth**...*" (Isaiah 47:15), which corresponds to what John prophesies in our text:

> *"And the ten horns which you saw, and the beast, these will hate the harlot and will make her desolate and naked, and will eat her flesh and will **burn her up with fire**."*
> (Revelation 17:16)

In other words, both Isaiah and John are prophesying that this *Harlot Babylon* will meet her final destruction coming at the hands of those who were her allies, or her partners in her immorality, who had been seduced by her. Interestingly, the Hebrew word used by Isaiah, here translated *"trafficked,"* is also translated "traders" by J.P. Green (Green, Jay P., <u>The Interlinear Hebrew-Aramaic Old Testament</u>, Vol. III of The Interlinear Hebrew-Greek-English Bible, 2nd ed., Hendrickson Publishers, Peabody MA, 1985.). And it is also rendered "commercial, customer, customers, merchant, merchants..." in the Hebrew Aramaic Dictionary of the <u>New American Standard Exhaustive Concordance of the Bible</u> (New American Standard Exhaustive Concordance of the Bible, Hebrew-Aramaic and Greek Dictionaries, ed. by Robert L. Thomas, Th.D., Holman Bible Publishers, Nashville, 1981.). Nouns which are derived from this root word "sachar," include commerce, gain, market, merchandizing, and profit.

Perhaps even more interesting are the renderings for this word included in the Gesenius' Lexicon, related to this passage in Isaiah: "Metaph. *to have intercourse* with anyone, Isa. 47:15." (Tregelles, Samuel Prideaux , LL. D., <u>Gesenius' Hebrew and Chaldee Lexicon to the Old Testament Scriptures</u>, Mott Media, Milford, MI, 1979.). Hence we even see the sexual connotation of adultery, metaphorically speaking. How perfectly this corresponds to what is described in Revelation seventeen and eighteen as the relationship between Babylon the Harlot, and the kings and merchants of the earth. Thus there can be little doubt as to whether or not **Isaiah is prophesying about the same thing that John is writing about**, especially since both specifically refer to her as "***Babylon***," and are describing her ultimate destruction. It also points to what is discussed in the following, the "Economic Aspect of the Harlot Babylon."

The Political versus the Ecclesiastical or Religious Elements

Up to this point we have been seeing Islam as a major element in identifying what the Beast will be. Indeed the nations which now make up the Mesopotamian area, which are the former empires that were predicted by Daniel and have already come and fallen, are now all Islamic. But, unlike the glory days of the Muslim empires under the Umayyad dynasty or more recently the Ottoman Turks, the governments of some of these modern descendants are not so much ecclesiastical religious figures such as Caliphs and Imams, but mostly secular political leaders (Iran being a notable exception with powerful Ayatollahs). Some have kings (such as Saudi Arabia) and others have elected presidents and prime ministers. They are still Muslims, Islamists, but they are political more than religious. The religion of Islam is very powerful in those states, and the politicians could not come to power or maintain it without being (or professing to be) Islamists. But as we have seen in several of those countries, Islamic religionists and extremists have been to varying degrees restrained and regulated by the elected political governments. Turkey is a good example where under the leadership of the secular leader known as Ataturk the Sultanate was abolished in 1921, and the Caliphate in 1924. More recently Egypt's military deposed and executed an extremist Muslim leader from the Muslim Brotherhood in 2013, even though he had been elected as their President. During the "Arab Spring" of 2010 to 2012 it appeared as though the Islamic extremists and religionists would take over in a number of those mid-eastern nations, including Egypt and Syria. However, the extremists failed to gain and/or maintain power, and the secularists are back in control.

This recent and present trend could of course change and may be changing. Many Bible scholars see Islam as the Beast and the Antichrist as an Islamic religious figure, such as an Ayatollah or Caliph or Imam, probably claiming to be the long awaited Mahdi or Twelfth Imam. In fact there seems to be a paradigm shift in eschatological thinking among futurists. More and more scholars are seeing the fact that Islam and those Mesopotamian Islamic nations are a much better match for the Beasts of Daniel and Revelation, than any Revived Roman Empire in the form of either the European Union, or the Roman Catholic Church (see authors such as Joel Richardson, or Walid Shoebat). And indeed, when one examines the eschatological teaching of some Islamist it does make a lot of sense, as an Islamic religious leader with power like the former Ayatollah Khomeini, and his successor Ayatollah Ali Khamenei, "Supreme Leaders" in Iran, may present themselves as the Mahdi, or the Twelfth Imam. It also seems possible that Islamic extremism may win the day in the middle-east, * and the ultimate leader may indeed be such an Islamic religious figure. But, if such is to be the case it would seem that the distinction John makes between the Beast and the Harlot Babylon is misleading at best. It is especially confusing to have the Beast then attacking and destroying the Harlot - that would be an Islamic cleric destroying his own religion. Such is possible, but doesn't seem at all probable, nor consistent with John's symbology.
*[As of this writing the movement known as Islamic State Iraq and Syria (ISIS) has been very much in the news, with their extensive

incursions taking parts of Iraq and Syria. Iran (Shia) either has, or is on the verge of acquiring nuclear weapons, and while opposed to ISIS (Sunni) is also spreading their brand of militant Islamic extremism around the globe. As it appeared recently such radical religious versions of Islam may be winning - time will tell.]

What may be more consistent with this prophecy with a Beast, or beasts, and a rider called The Harlot Babylon, would be a political leader over a coalition of initially ten states or nations. He will be Islamic but his government will be more secular, like most of the national leaders today. He may deceive the Islamists into believing that he is the Mahdi, * but once he sets himself up as god (Allah) they will rebel against him and he will then destroy them with his military might. Furthermore, it may well be that there will be a reaction against the current wave of Islamic extremism in the form of world-wide terrorism, even in the Islamic community. ** This may mean that the leader who will emerge and successfully pull together a coalition of ten Islamic nations, will do so under the banner of Moderate, peaceful Islam. Such a leader would initially be seen as a savior to the whole world, including what is now war-torn Islamic countries in which the victims are mostly Muslim as the various sects fight against each other. Such a leader would be a uniter to bring them all together under one Islamic banner, consolidating their combined power both economically (largely controlling the world's most vital resource - oil), and militarily (who else would ever use their weapons, especially weapons of mass destruction (WMD)?).

*[There are several different beliefs and definitions about this messiah figure known as "the Mahdi." Some Islamist theologians don't believe in it at all. Some believe he will just be an ordinary man. Most Shia, believe he already exists and is being hidden away (called Occultation) until the right time for him to be revealed. Some, known as "Twelver Shia," believe he will be the "Twelfth Imam." Most Sunnis believe he is Mohammed's successor and his coming is still future, and some believe he will establish a Caliphate.]

**[This is a dynamic rapidly evolving situation. As of this writing there are riots in Iran wanting to reform their government. Isis seems to be in its death thralls with the current administration in the U.S. taking an active leadership role in combating such Islamic terrorism, and even in opposing the regime in Iran. Saudi Arabia has a new king, and is in opposition to the Iranian regime as well, more or less allied with the west.]

Babylon the Great

Once we have unraveled the part of the "mystery," as John calls it, with respect to the symbology of the Harlot as representing the religious element, the next question is what does Babylon represent? What does the city of Babylon have to do with the religious element?

First it might be noted that the very name "Babylon" translated into English means "gate of God." Secular historian, Geoff Simons credits "religious commitment" with "stimulating innovations in architecture, imaginative mythology, and social organization" in the Mesopotamian area by as early as 4000 BC (Simons, Geoff, Iraq, From Sumer to Saddam, St. Martin's Press, New York, NY, 2nd edition, 1996, p. 114). He then proceeds to articulate the developments in these early civilizations which became "Babylon," from which one can easily detect the overarching influence of their religious beliefs as the organizing principle in the evolution of their cultures. Rev. Alexander Hislop, in his book The Two Babylons, traces the continuous thread in the evolution of religious err all the way back to Nimrod and his father Cush, the son of Ham and grandson of Noah (see note * for more on this). According to the biblical record (Genesis 10:8-11), Nimrod was the founder of Babel, or Babylon, and built Ninevah in Assyria as well. Thus, we know that historically speaking **"Babylon" is identifiable not only with a geographic region, an ancient empire, and an ethnic heritage, but is equally identifiable with a false religious system.**

*[Although Rev. Hislop's conclusions are clearly debatable, in that the Roman Catholic Church is probably not the "Babylon" of Revelation, he has unearthed some very interesting connections between the various false religious beliefs that seem to have evolved from the early goddess Semiramus, or Rhea, and her husband/son Ninus, who in the form of the son was also known as Bacchus, or Tammuz. Rev. Hislop shows the correlation between Semiramus and Ninus, and the Egyptian Isis and Osiris. He also traces Ninus, and Tammuz or Bacchus to Nimrod ("the mighty hunter of Genesis 10:9), and the father of Ninus to Bel, or Belus, which he concludes must have been Cush. He then traces these same pagan concepts forward to

show their counterparts in Greek mythology, and even in modern Roman Catholicism.]

However, the question still remains, what is the connection between Babylon and the much more recent religion of Islam? It would seem that Islam is more associated with Mecca, or Medina (Mohammed's home town), or even Jerusalem where the Dome of the Rock stands on the supposed* Temple Mount.

*["Supposed" temple mount because it has now been as much as proven that it is not the site of any of the Jewish temples, but is the remains of the Roman Fortress known in antiquity as Fort Antonia - see <u>Temple - Amazing New Discoveries that Change Everything about the Location of Solomon's Temple,</u> by Robert Cornuke.]

First, while we see Islam as the current embodiment of the Harlot, she is not the sum total of all that the Harlot represents. We must remember that this harlot is riding the seven-headed beast. Since the seven heads represent all the empires back to the original Babylonian Empire, Hammurabi's empire, the Woman or Harlot also goes all the way back to that earliest empire. It is not just a religion associated with any one of those empires, or just the last form of the empire, but false religion in general which spans the ages beginning with the earliest Babylonian religion. Now this might not seem to make much sense at first, until one takes a close look at these false religions that have evolved over millennia, one morphing into the other and eventually into what is known today as Islam.

Beginning with the early Babylonian god, Marduk or Bel (or Belus, Latin) was supposed to be the founder of Babylon, and the father of Ninus. Ninus was the actual builder and first king of the Babylonian monarchy, and is identified with the biblical Nimrod (Genesis 10:8-11). Similarly, "Nebo" (or Nabu) another Babylonian god, which was also worshipped by the Assyrians, is also traced back to Cush, who Rev. Hislop identifies as "the ringleader in the scheme for building the great city and tower of Babel" (Hislop, Rev. Alexander, <u>The Two Babylons - or The Papal Worship,</u> p. 26). Numerous scholars find this same deified character in the Egyptian Thoth, and Hermes in the Greek, and Mercury in Latin.

Thus going back to the very beginnings of the world's major false religions and idolatry, we see it began with Cush,

the cursed grandson of Noah. Hence, it takes us all the way
back to the original city of Babylon and the tower of Babel
described in the Bible (Genesis 11). Furthermore, Hislop shows
that the principle Babylonian Deities, Semiramus and her
husband/son Ninus (which are counterfeits of the Biblical
Virgin Mary and God the Father who also becomes God the
Son in Jesus) also show up in most of the other major religions
pursuant to the Babylonian/Chaldean religion:

> "From Babylon the worship of Mother and the Child spread
> to the ends of the earth. In Egypt, the Mother and the Child
> were worshipped under the names of Isis and Osiris. In
> India, even to this day, as Isi and Iswara; in Asia, as Cybele
> and Deoius; in Pagan Rome, as Fortuna and Jupiter-puer, or
> Jupiter, the boy; in Greece, as Ceres, the Great Mother,
> with the babe at her breast, or as Irene, the goddess of
> Peace, with the boy Plutus in her arms; and even in Thibet,
> in China, and Japan, the Jesuit missionaries were astonished
> to find the counterpart of Madonna and her child as
> devoutly worshipped as in Papal Rome itself; ..."
> (Hislop p. 20).

Thus according to Hislop we have a very idolatrous system
of religious heresy, which transcends time and history with
respect to succeeding world empires. It is the original
counterfeit and perversions of the truth which Satan used Cush
and Nimrod to conceive and propagate, right after God started
over with the global deluge of the Noahic flood. It is initially
associated with the city of Babylon and the biblical tower of
Babel, and the earliest forms of what became the Babylonian
religion.   Since then it has been passed on from civilization to
civilization, generation after generation, and **exists in modern
times in a modified form in what we know as the religion of
Islam.**

Although Islam features the monotheistic god, "Allah,"
even Allah seems to be descended from the ancient Sumerian
and Babylonian moon god. Renowned historian Will Durant
writes:

> "Within the Ka'aba, in pre-Moslem days, were several idols
> representing gods. One was called Allah; three others were

Allah's daughters, al-Uzza, al-Lat, and al-Manat. We may judge the antiquity of this Arab pantheon from the mentions of Al-il-Lat (Al-Lat) by Herodotus (fifth century B.C. Greek historian) as a major Arabian deity. The Quaraish paved the way for monotheism by worshipping Allah as chief god ..." (Will Durant, <u>The Story of Civilization - The Age of Faith</u>)

From archeological evidence we see that Allah was considered the chief god among many others, long before Mohammed arrived on the scene. Mohammed simply proclaimed him to be the only god, but actually retained many of the pagan rituals and symbols associated with him, such as **the crescent moon** (the current symbol of Islam which was the symbol of the Babylonian moon god), kissing the Black Stone, and praying toward Mecca. **Thus we have an element of commonality and a thread of continuity that is present in the evolution of major world religions from Babylon of Cush and Nimrod's time down to the Babylon of today with its Islamic religious system.**

In his book Rev. Hislop seems to make a strong case for the Roman Catholic Church being the Harlot because of the perversions of beliefs and practices which resemble and seem to be influenced by the Babylonian idolatries and heresies. However such an interpretation is not consistent with all the facts given in scripture (as discussed above). Nor is it consistent with what is actually developing in our world today. Joel Richardson's Islamic Antichrist (discussed and quoted above) would be much closer to fulfilling the prophecies concerning this Woman, the Harlot Babylon. However, what would seem to be even more consistent with both scripture (if we pay attention to the details), and present global developments and trends, is to see Islam as the religion or religious element symbolized by the Harlot Babylon, which rides the Beast (the Political and Military element) to power. It is even possible that this ultimate world religion would bring together not only Islam, but Spiritism, and the various forms of New Age religious beliefs, to follow the Antichrist. And in fact it is not inconceivable that it would be tolerant enough to include the apostate Christian church (apostate Catholicism as well as liberal Protestantism). More on this in the discussion about the nature of the Antichrist.

The point here is that Babylon seems to be mostly symbolic of the apostate religious element, which of course affects and is enmeshed with every other aspect of the cultures involved. Once again, we see that it is coming full circle - it all started in those early post-deluge Mesopotamian cultures, and that is where it will all end, according to Bible prophecy. What we see today in our world are developments that certainly appear to be headed in exactly that direction. If we are realistic in assessing the situation and present trends, the only viable candidate to become the dominant religious power intimately associated with an emerging political and military power, would be Islam in its relationship to most of the Islamic states in the middle-eastern Mesopotamian area. Islam is riding on the back of the secular governments of those states. However, she gets her real power from the people - what John's prophecy refers to as *"many waters"* (Revelation 17:1), which he interprets for us as *"peoples and multitudes and nations and tongues"* (17:15). As we saw in the overthrow of the former Shah of Iran, the people are almost unanimously Islamic and will depose even a powerful leader who is not Islamic enough for them, and may even replace him with a religious cleric, such as the Ayatollah Khomeini. Truly Islam sits on the multitudes of the people as its power base, and rides on the back of the political governments in what is a two-way, symbiotic, reciprocal relationship - each needing and benefiting the other.

However, as we have also noted in making the distinction between the Harlot Babylon and the Beasts, the latter turns against the former, and "devours" her:

> *"16And the ten horns which you saw, and the beast, these will hate the harlot and will make her desolate and naked, and will eat her flesh and will burn her up with fire."*
> *(Revelation 17:16)*

Again, as discussed above, it seems unlikely that an Islamic cleric, as an Ayatollah, or an Imam or Caliph, would turn against and destroy his own religion - though it is of course not impossible. Similarly, it seems rather improbable that an

Islamic extremist would end up destroying his own religion about which he had been fanatical, once he came to power - unless he was faking it all along, which is also always a possibility. It does seem more likely that a political figure may come to power who, like Sadaam Hussein and most of those in power in those Islamic countries today, will be to some degree quite secular in their approach to governing, while at the same time Muslim. Such a leader will likely be more motivated by his lust for power and control, i.e. political ambitions, than truly committed to the advancement of the religion of Islam. Indeed, according to several of the predictions we have looked at, he eventually claims to be god himself, and John tells us he requires everyone to take his mark and worship him. This is not at all consistent with Islamic theology, or eschatology for that matter, which have always made their monotheism the major mark of distinction of their religion, and that one god is Allah. To them for any person on this earth to claim to be Allah would be intolerable blasphemy. Yet this is exactly what this eighth beast, the Antichrist, will do.

When he does this, his original power base, the Harlot Babylon, the multitude of followers of Islam, will rise up in rebellion against him. But by this time he will have gained control over the global economies of the world (Revelation 13:16-17). He will have unlimited wealth, and intimidating military power - probably including nuclear capability and other WMD (weapons of mass destruction). He may well be seen as the savior to the world by either having ended, or still promising to end the threat of Islamic terrorism by Islamic extremists. He will make a treaty of some kind with Israel, involving a non-aggression pact (this will be the peace that the West has been trying to negotiate for much of the last century). With the backing of the non-Islamic world he may even claim that he has to rid the world of Islamic extremists and terrorists. Under this banner he will crush those who rebel against his authority and claim to deity, in particular the Islamists.

However, according to Daniel 9:27 and Revelation 11:2 and 13:7 & 15, he will also break his treaty with Israel, and will go after both Jews and Christians to persecute and eliminate them, as they too will not submit to his demands to worship him, and to take his mark, the famed 666. In fact, as Daniel predicts, he *"will devour the whole earth and tread it down and crush it" (Daniel 7:21b) and "he will enter countries, overflow them and pass through. [41]He will also enter the Beautiful Land, and many countries will fall ... " (Daniel 11:40d-41)*.

In the last few verses of this 17th chapter of Revelation we are told that God uses the Beast to pour out his judgment on this Harlot, Babylon. The 18th chapter of Revelation goes on to give us more of the details about this fall of Babylon. One of the details that we learn about her from this 18th chapter is the fact that she will also be a world power economically.

The Economic Aspect of the Harlot Babylon

About the fall of Babylon, John writes in Revelation:
*""Fallen, fallen is Babylon the great! She has become a dwelling place of demons and a prison of every unclean spirit, and a prison of every unclean and hateful bird. [3]For all the nations have drunk of the wine of the passion of her immorality, and the kings of the earth have committed acts of immorality with her, and **the merchants of the earth have become rich by the wealth of her sensuality**." (Revelation 18:2-3 emphasis added)*

"[11]And the merchants of the earth weep and mourn over her, because no one buys their cargoes any more— [12]cargoes of gold and silver and precious stones and pearls and fine linen and purple and silk and scarlet, and every kind of citron wood and every article of ivory and every article made from very costly wood and bronze and iron and marble, [13]and cinnamon and spice and incense and perfume and frankincense and wine and olive oil and fine flour and wheat and cattle and sheep, and cargoes of horses and chariots and slaves and human lives. [14]The fruit you long for has gone from you, and all things that were luxurious and splendid have passed away from you and men will no longer find them. [15]The merchants of these things, who became rich from her, will stand at a distance because of

*the fear of her torment, weeping and mourning, [16]saying,
'Woe, woe, the great city, she who was clothed in fine linen
and purple and scarlet, and adorned with gold and precious
stones and pearls; [17]for in one hour such great wealth has
been laid waste!' And every shipmaster and every passenger
and sailor, and as many as make their living by the sea,
stood at a distance, [18]and were crying out as they saw the
smoke of her burning, saying, 'What city is like the great
city?' [19]And they threw dust on their heads and were crying
out, weeping and mourning, saying, 'Woe, woe, the great
city, in which all who had ships at sea became rich by her
wealth, for in one hour she has been laid waste!'"
(Revelation 18:11-19)*

As with many if not most cities that became great cities of
renown, and capital cites of nations and empires, Babylon was
strategically located for commerce and trade. According to the
<u>Funk and Wagnall's New Encyclopedia</u> (1983) she was
situated "astride the main overland trade route connecting the
Persian Gulf and the Mediterranean." She was a port city on the
Euphrates, lying between the Euphrates and the Tigris Rivers.
Under King Hammurabi of the first Babylonian Empire, she
became the most important city in the world, the capital city,
administrative and religious center, as well as the commercial
center of the empire. She was destroyed by the Assyrian
Sennacherib, but rebuilt and restored by his son Esarhaddon,
and then again became the capital city of the Neo-Babylonian
Empire under King Nebuchadnezzar. She even maintained
much of her importance under the Persian rulers, Cyrus and his
successors up to Xerxes, who made it their capital city as well.
Some historians even tell us that Alexander the Great made it
his capital for a time.

Today there is not much left of the original city, but
Sadaam Hussein began a restoration of parts of it, especially
Nebuchadnezzar's palaces. * Since Sadaam it has been
developed as a tourist site. For John's prophecy to be fulfilled
literally, the city will have to be rebuilt and again become
something like the capital city of the future empire of the Beast,

or of the Harlot, Islam. When we see this happening, we better take special notice.

*[The most important of the standing monuments of Babylon today are the Summer and Winter Palaces of King Nebuchadnezzar II, the Ziggurat attached to it, the Street of Processions, the Lion of Babylon, and the famous Ishtar Gate.]

However, the implication of all this seems to be that the religious element has been, and will again be, important to the world commercially. It is interesting that Mohammed was born into a merchant family and was himself first involved in his uncle's business as a trader. Some believe that he himself may have even been a camel driver on caravans to Syria. Historians tell us that aside from violent conquest, Islam was spread around parts of the world through trade - i.e. commerce.

Today Islamic countries are at the same time some of the richest, and the poorest in the world. Because they are rich in the most precious resource in the world, **oil,** Sheiks and Oil Barons and some of the governments of those Islamic nations are incredibly rich, and getting more so every day. While the majority of the common people may not share in much of the wealth, there is apparently a trickle down effect, at least to some. The rest of the world is waking up to the huge potential of the middle-eastern markets. Products are being designed and produced and marketed specifically to the Islamic consumers, including financial instruments that are billed as Sharia compliant.

Consider these shocking revelations from as early as 2008: "Islamic finance has rapidly emerged as one of the most dynamic segments of the global financial services industry and is today a global phenomenon. There are Islamic finance institutions operating in over 75 countries and with assets estimated at around US$700 billion, a figure which is growing at a rate of about 15% a year. With a May 2008 report declaring that approximately **$4 trillion was available for investment in the Middle East, Islamic separatism in the form of sharia finance has become a big business--with Western financial institutions** hurrying to get in on it by accommodating Muslims in setting up parallels financing structures in the West...." (Robert Spencer, Stealth Jihad, 2008; pp. 182, 185, 187)

"Islamists are attempting to impose Shariah Compliant Finance (SCF) on Western institutions to use our own financial strengths against us. The most serious problem with SCF is that it legitimates and institutionalizes Shariah law (i.e., Islamic law), a theo-political-legal doctrine violently opposed to Western values. **With $1-$2 trillion petrodollars annually looking for an investment home, blind exuberance is driving financial institutions to adopt SCF, without even a minimal baseline for legal compliance.** This willful blindness, and lack of both transparency and due diligence may cause SCF to be the next sub-prime crisis, but this time with deadly consequences." ("What is Shariah Law - National Security and Financial Risks"; Shariah Finance Watch at http://www.shariahfinancewatch.org).

Most of the items mentioned in John's prophecy cited above, over which the rest of the world will mourn, are luxury items, as opposed to essentials like grain and meat. And it is the merchants who will be most affected, especially the shipping lines - i.e. world trade. According to the prediction, the world will not be mourning the loss of those items mentioned, but the loss of the markets for those items. Certainly the Middle-Eastern Islamic world will be a major market, without which the global economies will suffer.

Thus Babylon, the Harlot, will be a major player in this final end-time global empire of the Beast and the Antichrist such that there will be somewhat of a symbiotic relationship between the woman and the beast almost until the end. It will not only be a powerful element religiously but economically as well. This Antichrist will try to eliminate the competition of the power of this religious element, the Harlot Islam, but it will be at great expense to the global economy - which may only help to consolidate his power as a global ruler. Nevertheless, the fact that Islam is already becoming both the religious and the economic player on the world's stage, much like the Harlot Babylon predicted by John, should get the rational thinking man's attention.

Furthermore, when we pay attention to the details of these predictions, the specificity greatly narrows the scope of who and what they are all about. How many candidates are there on the world stage that were around and powerful during the days of those early empires, the Babylonian, the Medo-Persian and the Alexandrian? What religions in existence today were already enmeshed and incestuously involved with those empires and their rulers, all the way back to the beginning of post-deluge false religions? Such details greatly limit the search criteria, and the winner is only too obvious.

Needless to say, it isn't the Roman Empire revived in the form of the European Union, which is making up a coalition of nations, which are connected with those early ancient empires. Nor is it the Roman Catholic Church, nor Apostate Christianity, which has been riding the Beast made up of all those ancient empires, and is still in power with them today. But the middle-eastern nations in that Mesopotamian region, and their religious counterpart Islam, seem to be a pretty good match.

Chapter 4 What Rational Intelligent Conclusions Can be Drawn?

Maybe, Just Maybe

The popular and often quoted definition of insanity is to keep doing the same thing that never works over and over again, hoping this time it will work. Based on this definition one must definitely conclude that the only problem with this world we live in is men - men who are obviously insane, by that definition.

Beginning with a realistic look at the global situation and developments in our world today we see a rapidly growing problem that logically spells disaster for many if not all of us - and that in the not so distant future. One need only tune into the nightly news or look on-line at current global developments to see what is happening. The realist - as opposed to pie-eyed utopians who like to wear rose-colored glasses that obscure their vision of what they don't want to see - can see clearly what is happening. To say they are concerned would probably be an understatement. What is probably most distressing is that most realists (which excludes many politicians running for office) have at least this nagging sense that that no one has a credible solution to the problem, or problems, which are looming larger every day.

Of course a major part of the real problem is that there is unwillingness, perhaps an inability, to even face the problem - to call it what it is. When the Political Correctness that rules the day in both our national and international politics, is determined to cast the blatantly obvious enemy of our whole way of life and our infidel worldviews, as nothing other than a peaceful religion, equal in merit to any other religion (as per Relativism and Multiculturalism) - "Houston, we have a problem!"

But even if we do fully recognize the problem, what are we going to do about it? How do we solve it? Will diplomacy persuade the wild-eyed fanatics, who are terrorizing our world today, to give up their cause, their fanaticism, and their deeply held religious beliefs? Do we play "lets make a deal" with people whose religion tells them it is perfectly right and pleasing to their god (Allah) to lie to and make deals with infidels, which they have no intention of keeping - people who have a pretty perfect record of doing just that? With a host of people who openly proclaim their absolute hatred of us and all that we stand for, and whose goal is to either eliminate us, or subdue us, forcing their religion and Sharia Law on all of us, will being nice and tolerant change their hearts? Even if we are only talking about a minority of those who adhere to that religion, we are talking about a very militant, determined and violent army of millions of suicidal, homicidal terrorists, and their numbers keep growing.

Alternatively, will we solve this militarily? Do we start bombing and fighting about at least a fifth of the world's population? If we openly attack one Islamic group or country, as we did in Iraq, won't that just mobilize others to join in the fight against us? Or, if we take "boots on the ground" off the table, as is clearly the position of most western leaders and apparently the will of the populace and electorate, what can we really accomplish? If we were to use nuclear weapons - which isn't even being considered - would that bring an acceptable solution? Wouldn't that provoke the other nuclear powers, such as Russia and China and North Korea, to join in the conflagration? Who would win in a nuclear world war?

Maybe someone would like to suggest that the United Nations will be the solution, or will come up with a solution - if they want to hear a roar of laughter from the adults in the room. Maybe the time for optimism has come and gone. The Texicans and Davey Crocket and Jim Bowie who fought bravely to defend the Alamo were optimistic to the end - how did that work out for them? * Accurate assessment of the real-world situation, knowing the enemy and the threat, and determining a course of action based on that information, trumps optimism and even bravery, or wonderful intentions, every time.
*[Granted the cause they fought for eventually won out, but it took a lot more than naïve optimism to save Texas from Santa Anna.]

The point is, we are as a world, as a global community, in desperate straits, whether we know it, or can recognize it, or will admit it, or not. And the fact of the matter is that time is running out - the longer it goes on the more irreversible it becomes. **So, when it becomes obvious that men don't have any viable solutions, maybe it is time to consider looking somewhere else? Maybe when it comes to global developments it is not so naïve, or unsophisticated, or illogical, to at least consider looking to a source that has a well established, proven record of being accurate and reliable. Maybe,** the smart guys, the wise men of this world, who have allowed us to get into this mess, should be seen for what the Bible says they are - "fools" (God's word, not mine - Psalms 14:1, 1 Corinthians 1:20 & 3:18), the blind leading the blind (Matthew 15:14). Maybe, unlike our predecessors down through the annals of history, we should learn from that history.

Unlike our human leaders, God doesn't make mistakes. What God has revealed, through the ancient prophets like Daniel and John, has always been accurate - profoundly so - down to today. **Maybe** what certainly looks like their predictions coming true, is just that. <u>**Maybe, just maybe**</u> **men ought to at least be informing themselves on what God has revealed about the last days, and then looking realistically at what is going on in our world.** Then based on that information, knowledge of the relevant facts, they could reach rational conclusion and make decisions about what we can or need to do.

What Are We Looking For?

While the world (i.e. the unbelievers) are looking for world peace, and most of the world's leaders today believe that it will only come through a one-world government, that just might not be too realistic. Of course world peace could be attained easily enough, if everyone will just lay down their arms, and submit to Islam, and their government, and their Shariah Law. However, **if there exists anyone insane enough to think or hope that it will be Islam that will lay down their arms, and give up their god-ordained destiny to dominate and rule the planet - good luck with that**. Ever heard of "Allah-Akbar"?

However, one world government will be possible, and become a reality - according to a literal understanding of biblical prophecy. Guess who will rule? Will it be the liberal progressives? The Christians? The Catholics or the Pope? The Americans or the Europeans? Russia or China? All of these are candidates for the job, right? But a half-way intelligent assessment of the current realities might just guide one to some more reasonable answers.

Who controls most of the world's most valuable and essential resource, oil? Who is completely committed to gain control over the world no matter what the cost, no matter how they have to go about it? Who is it that is on the move today to accomplish that goal, and too often encountering little meaningful opposition except within their own ranks? Who has become virtually untouchable because of global Political Correctness? Who has leaders that are strong, and totally committed to their cause and beliefs, and are not to be deterred from accomplishing their clearly proclaimed goals - elimination or dominance of all "infidels"? Who has been able to deceive the whole world into believing that they aren't really a threat, in spite of their hostile, violent, militaristic, terroristic actions to the contrary?

Duh! Let's see, is it America, the Christians, the Catholic Church, or the o so powerful and threatening European Union? Is it China who desperately needs foreign oil and western markets for their products? Is it Russia - who also desperately needs foreign markets and high prices for their oil for economic survival? Oh scenarios can be imagined, and of course are being proposed, which have Russia or China as the likely suspects, but if they were going to do it they should have done it before the Islamists became so strong. Even they have no answers to the Islamic terrorism threats in their own countries, or around the rest of the world, other than the nuclear solutions - which would be somewhat suicidal for them, and they know it. Besides that, Russia is one of the Islamists best allies, as they are profitable markets for Russia's products, especially military armament.

But let's say we still don't really have a clue, or just can't figure it out. So maybe we should consider what the Bible predicts (since it has been incredibly accurate so far). Here are some of the clues we are given between Daniel and Revelation:

- We have a coalition of initially ten nations - a ten-horned beast, coming up out of the sea of humanity (or possibly the Mediterranean area);
- A powerful leader emerges from that coalition by deception and intrigue, who is characterized by his boastful and blasphemous big mouth;
- The ten nations and their leader are associated in some integral way with the preceding empires in the greater Mesopotamian region going back to the Babylonian Empire (probably the first Babylonian Empire), and including at least the Medo-Persian and Alexandrian Empires;
- The coalition of nations are intimately related to and enmeshed with a religious system, which is also a powerful political and economic entity (the "Harlot"):
- This religious system is also associated with the preceding empires, and have been a powerful element down through time beginning with ancient Babylon;
- That religious system is centered in the city of Babylon as its capital or center of operations and seat of government;
- Both the government of the coalition (the Beasts) and the religious element (the Harlot Babylon) are savagely opposed to Judaism and Christianity;
- The leader of the coalition (the Antichrist) makes a seven year peace treaty with Israel (probably a non-aggression pact), but breaks it after 3 ½ years, and takes the city of Jerusalem, desecrates the temple and stops the sacrifices;
- This leader has a prophet ("the false prophet") who proclaims him to be God and passes a global edict (probably a "fatwa") that everyone has to worship the image of the leader, and take his identification number

which in some way features three sixes (like all the bar codes we use today for inventory of everything);

- This coalition, or its leader, amazes the whole world by making a seemingly miraculous recovery from a mortal wound;
- Once in power this leader goes on a rampage slaughtering his enemies;
- Eventually the religious element falls victim to his lust for power and control, after he asserts himself as the only god to be worshipped;
- He apparently moves his capital or base of operations and control to Jerusalem, after destroying Babylon and the religious element centered there;
- He goes into Egypt to conquer and pillage (Egypt is apparently not part of his coalition, or else rebels against his authority and control);
- He responds to rumors probably of insurrection back in the North and the East (possibly Israel and Iraq) and returns to the valley of Jezreel, also called the valley of Jehoshaphat, or the valley of HarMagedon (Armageddon), where he marshals all his forces;
- Like Napoleon of old, it is there he meets his Waterloo - he is wiped out by the "Lamb on the white horse," and His legions of followers.

What Are We Seeing in our World Today?

What we have already on the world's stage are all the pieces, the cast and props we need for the dramatic story and scenes described by the prophets to be played out. It actually looks as if the movie has already begun. We have the beasts - at least ten and currently more than ten nations, in the greater Mesopotamian area, which are the natural descendants of all of the former empires named by Daniel, going back to the original Babylonian Empire. Today there are in that area Turkey, Syria, Jordan, Lebanon, Iraq, Saudi Arabia, Yemen, Oman, United Arab Emirates, Qatar, Bahrain, Kuwait, and Iran. Surrounding them we have several more countries including Egypt, Sudan and Libya to the South West, Pakistan and Afghanistan to the East, along with several former Soviet Union bloc countries that are largely Islamic. Those governments and leaders of those same nations are enmeshed with a very large and powerful religion - **Islam**. That religion has roots that go all the way back to the beginnings of anti-Judeo-Christian religions, the religion of the earliest Babylonians. The adherents of that religion have a fierce hatred for God's people Israel, and they are united in their intentions to rid the world of all Jews. They are also quite open and obvious about their hatred for Christians, professing to believe in a false Jesus who was just a man and did not die on the cross. Their leaders refer to the United States as "the Great Satan."

Those Islamic nations are all centered in the area now known as Iraq, and the ancient city of Babylon is at the geographic center of Iraq. Babylon has great historic significance, though it is today mostly still in ruins. However, Sadaam Hussein had begun a major restoration project, wanting to restore it to its former glory, and was trying to project himself as being the virtual reincarnation of Nebuchadnezzar the Great. Babylon has the romantic history, and is strategically and geographically located to become the center of a united Islamic empire.

As of this writing Iran is ruled by a militant Islamic extremist Ayatollah. Iran's leadership is belligerent, boisterous, extremely anti-Semitic and anti-Christian. Iranians are Persian, and modern day Iran is a direct descendant of the former Persian Empire. Iran is known universally as the biggest sponsor of terrorism around the world, feared even by their Islamic neighbors because of their expansionism and aggressive policies. She also is heavily armed, and is as of this writing believed to be very close to having a nuclear weapon, if she doesn't have one already. The United States is currently proving to be incapable of stopping her, though the recent leadership pretended to have reached an agreement to slow her down - and therein lies much of the problem. Those who could do something to stop her won't, either because of the lack of will, or the lack of desire to do so. And indeed, when the

Islamists do form a coalition of at least ten nations, the primary oil producing nations, the threat of cutting off oil imports to Europe, and the United States, will paralyze both with respect to any meaningful interventions, either economic (as in real sanctions) or militarily.

Some will argue that the US is no longer dependent on such foreign sources of oil, because in 2012-2013 she supposedly produced almost half of her consumption. How long can we survive as an economy, and a military power, on half of the oil we need now? Maybe Canada and Mexico will help us out and meet that other 50% instead of selling it on the world markets as they all do now - and maybe we better not hold our collective breath hoping that will happen. Maybe Russia or Argentina will come to our rescue - and maybe hell will freeze over before that will ever happen. People who are believing such optimistic propaganda are apparently unaware that our production only rose to those levels because the price of oil was high enough for the oil companies to make a profit from such expensive methods as Fracking and converting shale deposits into oil. Once our competitors (such as Saudi Arabia) manipulated the markets such that the price of oil dropped precipitously, those sources became no longer profitable and were shut down, as were our highly touted high production levels.

Perhaps the biggest threat is that the Islamic oil producing countries have the ability to manipulate the markets. Their consumption/production ratio is much lower than that of the US and her European allies, and they can increase or decrease production and raise or lower prices at will. Oil is the biggest weapon any one has today, in a world where opposing nuclear powers are paralyzed by fear of a nuclear holocaust, and rightfully so.

However, we do not yet see much of any kind of a coalition of these Islamic nations coming together. Instead, as of this writing we have Iran supporting insurrections, and rebels trying to topple other Islamic countries governments. At the same time we have seen ISIS (Islamic State of Iraq and Syria) trying to take over Iraq and Syria, and Iran fighting against ISIS and ostensibly supporting Syria. We have other nations in the region that are quite concerned about and feeling threatened by, and in opposition to both Iran and ISIS. We have a great divide in the whole Islamic world between the Shia and the Sunnis, who are fighting against each other. Then we have fighting between the militant extremists, and the moderates and secularists. At the present time we might be tempted to take comfort in this fact, that Islam is a divided house, and thus not really that much of a threat except for the threat of international terrorism. However, that very threat of terrorism and military expansionism is causing world opinion to turn against them.

In light of all this, how are we to believe that there will be a united coalition of ten of these nations, who will become dominated by one powerful leader, which will eventually dominate the world? Why should we take seriously what the Bible seems to be predicting as set forth in the preceding chapters? Consider the following facts and scenarios.

How Will it Happen?

First, according to a number of sources Sunnis makeup the majority of the Muslim population, about 85-90 %. Saudi Arabia, Egypt, Syria, and Turkey are mostly Sunni, while Iran, Iraq and Lebanon are mostly Shiite. ISIS however is led by Sunni Muslims (Salafi jihadi extremist). The Islamic community is further divided between those who are militant extremists, and the more moderate Muslims. During the Arab Spring of 2010-2012 the president of Egypt, Hosni Mubarak, was deposed and replaced by a leader of the Muslim Brotherhood, Mohamed Morsi. The Muslim Brotherhood is recognized in many if not most of the Islamic countries as a terrorist organization. Morsi was deposed in 2013 by the more moderate Islamists elements led by the military, who also led a brutal crackdown on the Muslim Brotherhood. It is perhaps this underlying struggle between the more militant, aggressive and terroristic elements in the Islamic world, and the more moderate Muslims, that is the most significant. The latter would rather be more patient and deceptive, and garner more support from the rest of the world through their propaganda campaign (ala the Palestinian cause against Israel), currying public sympathy for their cause. The cause and the goal of such moderates is exactly the same, world domination, but their methods are very different - and probably more productive in the long run.

It looked like the radical extremists were winning the day, back when the Arab Spring was in play. Still today it looks like the radical extremists may have the upper hand, between Iran and ISIS and so many other Islamic terrorist groups, except that they are fighting each other. A possible scenario is that these radical extremists elements will continue to grow and eventually become powerful enough to gain control over the governments of ten of those nations in the area. The question would seem to be which of the two major factions will be able to dominate? The Sunnis have a clear majority numerically. However, if Iran becomes a nuclear power, the balance may shift in her favor, and she may emerge as the dominant power to which the others may have to submit. If so she will do so mostly by sheer force.

Certainly in many respects an Iranian leader like she has now and has had recently, would fulfill many of the predictions in the Bible - one who is boisterous, belligerent, blasphemous, very anti-Semitic and anti-Christian - like the "little horn" of Daniel and John's prophecies. His coalition of ten Islamic nations in the greater Mesopotamian region with a close religious affiliation (Islam), would match much of what was predicted about this seven-headed ten-horned end-times beast, and its rider the Harlot Babylon.

However, there would seem to be a few details that don't exactly match the prophetic details. Daniel's "little horn," which is also the king of the North of Daniel 11 (the symbols used for the Antichrist), comes to power through deception and intrigue (Daniel 11:23-25), not initially through military conquest and bloodshed. Another related prophecy by John seems to give us an order in which these developments will happen, using the symbology of the Seals, and four horsemen. The second of the four horsemen is indeed a rider on a red horse, which we are told symbolizes *"tak[ing] peace from the earth, and that men should slay one another."* We are told there that *"a great sword was given to him"* (Revelation 6:4).

However, this is preceded by a *"white horse"* and its rider just has a bow, and is given a crown, and he then conquers the others. But while the red horse symbolizes bloodshed, the *"white horse"* would seem to symbolize more what Daniel described, coming to power and initially conquering by peaceful means such as deception and intrigue. We also know from Daniel 9:27 that this same ruler will make a seven-year peace treaty, or a non-aggression pact with Israel, which he will keep for 3 ½ years. Thus we may have another scenario that not only fits these details of biblical predictions more accurately, but also may make more sense in terms of what is plausible. That scenario is as follows.

Virtually the whole world is coming under attack, or feeling threatened by radical Islamic terrorists. Thus they - the Islamists - are incurring the opposition, and in some cases the wrath of most of the rest of the world. The propaganda war that was being waged so successfully, especially against Israel and her allies in favor of the Islamists, especially in Palestine, is now experiencing reversals in world-wide opinion and support. The more aggressive Shiite Iran becomes the more she is alienating even her Islamic neighbors, with whom she should be forming alliances. However the vicious militancy of her opponents, such as the Sunni Islamic State (IS or ISIS), is similarly being seen more and more as a threat in the region. Furthermore, the secular governments of most of those Islamic nations in the area are also threatened by the Islamic extremism. Like Egypt, they are more likely to oppose such radical extremists than join them and support them. These dynamics don't allow for much hope for any meaningful alliance between these warring factions, unless…

The whole world is crying out for someone who can bring some semblance of peace to the region (Mid-East), or at least put a stop to the terrorism. The world wants to believe that Islam is basically a good religion, a peaceful religion, which is just being hijacked by the radical extremist element - and it has become politically incorrect to suggest otherwise. But the world is asking, where are the moderates, the peaceful Muslims, who will stand up against the "rogue" radical element, and put a stop to what they are doing.   What will happen if perhaps a charismatic figure emerges from that Islamic community, who champions the cause of the Islamists to gain their support, but condemns the violence of the militant radical terrorists? What if he enters the world stage by trying to unite the moderate Sunni community, and possibly even reaching out to the moderate Shiites, to do something about their common problem, and the threat the radical elements present to them all. Then having organized a resistance movement, a coalition of Arabic (and possibly some Persian) allies he appeals to the rest of the world, especially the western world, posturing himself as the solution to the world's most distressing problems, promising to end Islamic terrorism and expansionism. Combine this with a grandiose gesture of recognizing Israel's nationhood by agreeing to a seven-year peace treaty or non-aggression pact, would he not gain the full support of most of the rest of the world? Not only would he be seen by the world as a heroic figure, a savior of sorts, but he would probably be able to write his own ticket. In light of how the US has sent money and arms to whoever she hoped would do her dirty work in the region, and as of his writing has recently sent modern fighter aircraft to Egypt, who would doubt that she will arm and support such a leader making such grand promises, despite the fact that he is an Islamist, a Muslim.

With the backing of western military powers, such as US and Europe, who desperately need the oil he can promise them, how hard will it be for him to become the dominant figure in region - even if he is opposed by a nuclear Iran? Of course the reality is that Iran may also become part of his coalition, as there seems to be a strong undercurrent there of opposition to the extremist government of the Ayatollahs even now. With external pressure and support to the Iranian resistance it is not inconceivable that the regime could be toppled and replaced by the more moderate faction - or perhaps by this coalition leader himself. However, to accomplish this he may have to be able to bridge the differences between the Shias and the Sunnis. One possibility that is not inconceivable is that this might be accomplished by a grand deception - by claiming to be the

Mahdi to the Sunnis, and the twelfth Imam as well to the Shia. By his skill at deception, and manipulation, what Daniel calls "intrigue," he just might be able to bring the sects together under his leadership.

If he is able to pull together such a coalition of Islamic allies, and garner the support of the western world, primarily the US and Europe, he may actually be able to effectively suppress the radical elements, bring some semblance of peace to the region, and reduce the threat of Islamic terrorism globally. Then we will have a figure who will be hailed by the world as a true savior, a messiah figure. If Anwar Sadat who led the Yom Kippur war against Israel, could become highly praised and respected and awarded a share of the Noble Peace prize for engaging in negotiations which resulted in the Egypt-Israel Peace Treaty, imagine what a heroic figure this end-times leader will become. As John puts it,

> *"And the whole earth was amazed and followed after the beast; [4]they worshiped the dragon because he gave his authority to the beast; and they worshiped the beast, saying, 'Who is like the beast, and who is able to wage war with him?'"*
> *(Revelation 13:3-4)*

Part of how he will do this amazing feat may be by getting the various factions to focus on their real enemies - the "infidel," the Jews and the Great Satan. To them he will promise a universal caliphate governed by Sharia Law. He will unite them under the banner of all that Islam really stands for. To the rest of the world he will present himself as a very peace loving and tolerant Muslim, denying that he has ambitions to bring the whole world under submission to Islam. When caught by one or the other in his duplicitous lies he will merely explain that it is what he has to tell them to get them to cooperate in bringing peace and unity - the same lie will work for both sides. The only difference will be that to the one he is saying global peace by peaceful coexistence, to the other he will be saying global peace by Islamic domination.

Once this now world leader has established and consolidated his power in the Islamic world, and gained the credibility and support of the rest of the world, he will have free reign. By that time he will probably already have unprecedented military power. With his wealth he will have been able to buy modern weaponry including missiles and probably an air force from sources such as Russia, but he will have been given perhaps even more by the western allies, primarily the United States.* The latter will arm him to enable him to fight the radical extremists, the Islamic terrorist elements threatening our world today. Very likely he will have nuclear weapons, either by overtaking Iran, or purchasing them from Russia, or China or North Korea or Pakistan or India, or perhaps given to him by now western allies to fight against such elements as Iran. Combine his real threat as a nuclear power (who will actually use them) and the economic threat of controlling the global markets by manipulating oil production, prices and or distribution of the oil (cutting of her adversaries oil supply), he will indeed become the long sought after one-world government.

*[The United States always has been a major supplier of arms to what have eventually become here enemies in the middle-east. She will continue to arm what are now seen as her allies to combat Islamic terrorists groups and state sponsors of terrorism, such as Iran. This armament is going to Islamists, who will eventually join the forces of the Beast becoming enemies of the West.]

Once he has consolidated his global dominance as the president of the world he will set up a global economy, which will make perfect sense to almost everyone, in the interest of global peace. This economy will be a state-of-the-art computerized system, a system that will eliminate the scourge of such crimes as robbery and theft of people's money, or the specter of tax evasion. It will involve a digital inventory and control system utilizing the bar-code (UPC) system already in use universally around the world. The new innovation will be that every person who will be able to participate in this global economic system will receive an Identification number. This number will be burned into a tiny chip, which will probably be injected under the skin of the left hand and the forehead. The number will probably be in the form of a bar code, which will be used as a banking account number, the equivalent of a social security number, and all of a persons relevant data will be stored in computer memory under that number. The implants will allow the person to perform business transactions, much like a credit card without the risk of stolen cards, and stolen identity (so people will be told). Everyone will be required to enroll in such a system, and receive and use their implanted IDs, in order to engage in normal economic transactions. Paychecks from employers will be deposited electronically into their accounts under that ID number. Purchases will be made by passing a scanner over the persons hand, or forehead, and the amount will be electronically debited from their account. Taxes might be deducted or paid electronically, possibly automatically - there probably won't even be any need for filing tax forms. Of course the government will have complete oversight and control of everyone's accounts and economic activities - privacy rights will become an obsolete concept. The implications of such a system are terrifying to the freedom-loving individual - but they won't have much choice but to go along with it to survive. It will be sold as the price for peace and unity, a "united global community." The masses will be duped, until it is too late - much like what has happened in recent history in Germany, Russia, and China.

Then the "Dragon" which is in the form of the Beast, will show his true face. Contrary to all of his promises, and pretenses he will not be the tolerant benevolent dictator the world was looking for, and believed him to be. There will be pockets of resistance and rebellions around the world, which he will put down with the force of a ferocious beast just as he is depicted to be. This will involve bloodshed around the world such as the world has probably not seen in a long time, if ever before. He will break his treaty with Israel, invade Jerusalem, desecrate the temple and stop the sacrifices going on there. He will also shed his pretenses with respect to his professed religion of Islam. He will demand that everyone worship and obey him as God in human flesh. He will go after all those who do not submit to his new universal religion, in which he

replaces all other gods as the supreme god. Christians and Jews
in particular will be persecuted and beheaded.

Once he sets himself up as god the Islamists who put him
into power in the first place will turn against him. They will try
to expose him as a false god, saying that only Allah is God. He
will then use his military to crush them and their capital city,
Babylon. This is what is predicted several times in Revelation,
specifically in Revelation 17:16-18, and described in great
detail in the 18th chapter.

Egypt will also resist his dominance, and he will invade her
and crush her resistance as well. Apparently when Egypt falls
Libya and Sudan (which Daniel refers to as Ethiopia) will
follow suit in submitting to his dominance. However, it seems
that rumors of insurrection or resistance to the east and the north
will cause him to return to the area of his new capital city,
Jerusalem. He will gather and marshal all of his forces on the
huge plain of Megiddo and in the valley of Esdraelon (in the
Hebrew, Plain of Jezreel - a plain in northern Israel which
stretches from the Mediterranean near Mt. Carmel to the Jordan
River), where many famous battles have been fought down
through history. This will be the "battle of Har Magedon" of
John's prophecy in Revelation 16:16. It is there that he will
meet his fate, and will literally meet his maker, the sovereign
God of the universe. It is known in scripture as "the battle of
HarMagedon" (or Armageddon). That of course will be what is
known as "the second coming of Christ," when He returns to
earth with His armies to defeat His foes, judge the earth, the
Beast, and all of His followers. That will also be when He
establishes His earthly Millennial and eternal kingdom on a
newly created earth.

Yes But!

There are some "yes buts" to this proposed scenario. They
include other possible scenarios, which are limited only by the
amount of imagination involved in coming up with them. Then
there would seem to be some hurdles that would have to be
overcome, for the preceding scenario, and biblical predictions,
to become realities. For example, according to both Daniel and

John there will have to be a temple in Jerusalem where the Jews will be worshipping, and sacrificing animals on the altar. We are told that the Antichrist will desecrate that temple, stop the sacrifices, and set up his own image to be worshipped - what Daniel and Jesus referred to as "the abomination of desolation" (discussed in the preceding). This would seem to be a problem.

Not only is there no such temple in Jerusalem now, but the prospects of building one on what is believed to be the old temple site seems virtually impossible. As most people probably know, the "temple mount" is now the site of an Islamic Mosque known as "The Dome of the Rock." It is declared to be one of their most sacred sites, and they make it known that it would be considered an act of war against the Islamic world for the Jews to desecrate that site, let alone build a temple there. Even a very conservative Prime Minister like Benjamin Netanyahu is not about to challenge them on this and incur their wrath, as it would also cause their western allies to blame Israel for what would happen. So how will it ever happen that the temple will be built, without another probably very bloody war in the region?

This is actually a problem that has no basis in fact. While it is the traditional view that the Dome of the Rock site is also the ancient Jewish Temple Mount site, recent research and archeological evidence has revealed that such is not the case. The fact is that it is the site of the old Roman fortress known in antiquity as Fort Antonia. Robert Cornuke has thoroughly researched the subject. In his book, <u>Temple - Amazing New Discoveries that Change Everything about the Location of Solomon's Temple</u>, he presents what seems to be irrefutable biblical, historical, and archeological evidence to prove that the actual temple site is to the South of that Roman Fortress, in what was "the City of David." What this means is that once the Jews come to realize and accept this reality there is nothing to stop them from building that "third temple" on the actual site of the earlier temples.

[This is not, however, Mr. Cornuke's conclusion, as he believes that the Antichrist will actually allow the Jews to build their temple on the traditional Temple Mount site, where the Dome of the Rock is now. Though he doesn't tell us, it is likely that he perceives the Antichrist as being European, certainly not a Muslim, or it is doubtful that he would reach such a conclusion. It is inconceivable that a Muslim who becomes the Antichrist would allow the Jews to build their temple on that Muslim holy site. But it is believable that the Jews will erect one on the true site of the previous historic temples, once they accept the truths Mr. Cornuke and a few others have recently brought to light.]

When this happens, people had better sit up and take notice. The erection of a Jewish temple in the old "City of David" will again be one of those highly unlikely developments, which will be fulfillment of detailed prophecy. Fools will ignore it, or find explanations to avoid the rather obvious significance and meaning of it, as they have done and continue to do with all of fulfilled prophecy in the Bible. But for those who know, it will be a clear sign, and somewhat ominous sign, that the end is near.

However, even if or when the temple gets built, there are many other possible scenarios especially for the near term, that could make it look like the scenarios presented above are too pessimistic and will never happen. For example, we could have very conservative leader elected in the US like another Ronald Reagan. As of this writing the current president is Donald Trump, whose actions seem to be of a very conservative nature, reversing the disastrous trends of administrations of the last several decades. There is reason for optimism among conservatives that the dangerous trend toward accommodating the enemy and embracing globalism, might be at least impeded to some extent for the time being. Or we could see a strong and courageous leader emerge in Europe who could possibly even unite the European Union (though none would appear to be on the horizon at this time). If both were to come to power in the same era and work together to oppose the rise of Islam, it is conceivable they could at least delay the appearance of the Beasts of Revelation and Daniel. Or, if either the US or Europe could actually become independent of OPEC oil, the above scenario would at least in part seem improbable. This they could do either by discovering and accessing their own oil reserves, or finding other sources, or by reducing their own

demand enough to no longer need OPEC's supply. Of course
theoretically this could be done by a combination of
conservation and development of alternative sources of energy.
However these have proven to be less than promising despite
the high costs associated with them so far - certainly not the
near term answer to the current and rapidly developing world
situation. Furthermore the other scenarios while possible and
plausible, appear unlikely as of this writing.

Conflicting Interpretations

For many decades at least, many prophecy "experts" have
interpreted the same passages we have looked at in the
preceding, and come up with very different interpretations. In
fact one of the most popular interpretations among the futurists
in the 20th century was that the Beasts would be Russia.
Biblically this would seem to be rooted largely in the
interpretation of "*Rosh*" and "*Meshech*" mentioned in passages
such as Ezekiel 38-39 as actually referring to Russia and
Moscow respectively. This has been shown by several scholars
to be very poor exegesis of scripture involving very faulty logic.
Then we also see prophecies that tell us that the forces that will
come against Israel in the last days, will come form the north, or
as Ezekiel puts it, "*the remotest parts of the north.*" And
indeed, when we saw the Soviet Union becoming such an
economic and military powerhouse, threatening the whole
world with nuclear war, and spreading Communism, it looked
like they were on the right track. Even today, though the Soviet
Union has fallen apart, and Russia seems like less of a threat,
she is still a major world power and a threat to the rest of the
world. It is not inconceivable that she could still be the Beast of
Revelation, except for a few bothersome details.

First and probably the biggest problem with this
interpretation is that it represents the kind of Bible exegesis that
can only lead to inaccurate conclusions, at best. The Rosh and
Meshech and the invader from the far north of Ezekiel's
prophecy are the forces of the leader referred to as "*Gog of the
land of Magog.*" From what Ezekiel writes in those two
chapters (38-39) it is abundantly clear that he could not be

referring to any time frame either before or during the future time that is known as the Tribulation Period - unless one ignores or rewrites what Ezekiel clearly wrote (which many seem to do). We are told in those two chapters that Gog appears at a time when Israel will be **living securely in her land** in "*unwalled villages*." We are also told that the outcome of this great war will be that God will destroy this huge force both by causing them to fight against each other (imagine that - Arabs and Persians fighting each other), and by sending "*a torrential rain, with hailstones, fire and brimstone*" (Ezekiel 38:21-22). Then he tells us that from that time on God's name will be glorified never to be profaned again, both in Israel, and among the nations, and He will "*restore the fortunes of Jacob,*" and will "*have poured out the Spirit on the house of Israel*" (Ezekiel 39:7, 21-29). None of this fits in the time frames many assign to it, either before or during those days of Great Tribulation for Israel. To suggest that she will actually be living securely in her land just because the Antichrist makes a phony seven-year peace treaty with her (one more of many before it), which he breaks after 3 ½ years, and disarms her cities (tearing down extensive walls now present), is not all that believable. To say that the nations, or even the whole house of Israel will know and recognize the glory of God never to profane His name again, will happen any time before the second coming of Christ to judge the whole earth, is to simply ignore or rewrite what scripture so clearly tells us. To say that God is going to restore Israel and pour out His Spirit on her before or during the Tribulation Period, is to simply contradict those passages that describe that period. Furthermore, to suggest that the Gog of Ezekiel is about a major global conflict which is to happen during that Tribulation Period, as most of those scholars who hold to this interpretation do, is to maintain that such a major event is not even mentioned in the main book that describes that period - the book of Revelation.

One who is not very informed on this subject of these interpretations, or not indoctrinated into this school of thought, may immediately object to that last statement about Gog not appearing in Revelation. Clearly John does

tell us about Gog and Magog, and that huge army he will
assemble to march against God's people Israel. It is found in
Revelation 20:8-9. However, John also tells us exactly when
this huge global event will occur - "*when the thousand years
are completed*" and when "*Satan is released from his prison*"
(Revelation 20-:7). Anyone even slightly familiar with Bible
prophecy will immediately recognize this reference to the
thousand years as referring to the Millennial reign of Christ
on this earth, which follows immediately the seven-year
Tribulation Period and the second coming of Christ. Those
who hold to the view that the Gog of Ezekiel will appear
before or during the Tribulation period insist that this Gog
John wrote about is not the same Gog Ezekiel wrote about.
However, their reasons for insisting they are not the same
consist of pointing out that there are details in Ezekiel's two
chapters, or 52 verses, which are not found in John's very
brief mention of it in a total of two verses - Duh!

Other arguments presented to try to make this case
involve nothing more than circular reasoning - they say that
because Ezekiel is writing about a battle during the
Tribulation Period (their unproven conclusion, which now is
their starting assumption) John's Gog must be a different
Gog since it is happening after the 1000 year Millennial
reign of Christ on earth. The simple fact is that nothing John
tells us in those two verses is in any way incompatible with
what Ezekiel wrote in 52 verses, Ezekiel just gives us a
whole lot more detail. But the conditions Ezekiel describes,
and the results of this major global conflict, only fit in that
post-Millennial era. There is much more to be considered
on this important subject that is discussed in detail in
another book by this author entitled <u>Gog/Magog Revisited -
Modern Myths and Theories Versus Actual Biblical Prophecy</u>
(available as ebook on Amazon).

There is also another popular theory that confuses the Gog
of Ezekiel with the Antichrist of Revelation. There are however
a number of significant descriptive details which do lend
credence to this view, which probably makes it more viable than

the view discussed above. After listing some of these similarities one proponent of this view goes so far as to make the following assertion: "Because these are descriptions that can only be applied to the time of the return of Jesus and the establishment of His messianic kingdom, it is impossible that Gog and his armies are anything other than the Antichrist and his armies." (Richardson, Joel (2012-06-08). <u>Mideast Beast: The Scriptural Case for an Islamic Antichrist</u> (p. 166). Kindle Edition.)

Again however, this theory is fraught with difficulty beginning with the inattention to details in the related prophecies. First, if John (and for that matter Daniel) was really writing about Gog when he describes this Beast we call the Antichrist, why did he not also call him Gog, but then later in the twentieth chapter writes about a Gog which is not the same Gog - is God the author of such confusion? Furthermore, how believable is it that there are to be two separate major world figures with major international armies both by the same name Gog, both appearing in these end-times, both similar in every respect (as far as what is revealed in Revelation 20:8-9), but not the same Gog? The simple fact is that the details which fit both the Gog of Ezekiel and the Beast or Antichrist also fit the Gog mentioned by John in Revelation 20, to the extent that such details are mentioned there at all. They cannot possibly all be the same.

Like the others discussed above, Richardson and others most of whom seem to subscribe to the Islamic Antichrist view, fail to recognize that John in his two verses in chapter 20 is telling us very clearly when the Gog of Ezekiel's prophecy is going to appear - after the Millennium. Again, they also ignore some of the details such as the fact that Israel will certainly not be living securely in her land when the Antichrist surfaces and comes to power. That situation will only exist in Israel again, after the Tribulation Period is over, and the new heaven and earth is created (Revelation 20:8-13), and Christ sets up His perfect kingdom on this earth.

The fact is that Ezekiel 38-39 is also in a context where it belongs, that gives us indicators as to the timing of its future occurrence. The preceding chapters describe God's judgment on both Israel and the surrounding nations, Israel's restoration in her land when they will live "*secure on their land*" (Ezekiel 34:27), when they will also repent, and God says "I will put my Spirit within you" (Ezekiel 36:27). This is followed by a resurrection, a bodily resurrection described in specific detail in the 37th chapter. It is after that resurrection of the 37th chapter that we get these developments with Gog appearing and a huge multitude of the enemies of God's people in the 38th-39th chapters rebelling one last time against God. It is not coincidental that this order matches what we see in Revelation, leading up to and including chapter twenty. After God's universal judgment in the preceding chapters of Revelation, we see the Millennial reign of Christ appearing in the 20th chapter. This is followed by a resurrection of the unsaved dead (Revelation 20:5), coinciding with the release of Satan, followed by the Gog rebellion, and after that God's last and final judgment on earth and in heaven. This judgment involves not only Gog and his followers, but Satan and all ungodly unbelievers as well - the Great White Throne judgment (Revelation 20:11-15). It is hard to imagine how God could make it much clearer.

In order to accommodate the massive rebellion against God after the perfect Millennial age of Christ reigning on this earth, both the views discussed above have a problem explaining where such a large multitude of unbelievers would be coming from. Most, including Richardson, completely miss or ignore the resurrection of the "*rest of the dead*" of Revelation 20:5, or manipulate its timing or meaning, and instead theorize that they are actually coming out of the Millennial age. Despite clear descriptions of that age as a kingdom in which Christ reigns and all those in it are living in obedience to Him, an age of righteousness in which the inhabitants all have the Spirit of God in and upon them - they insist that there will many who only outwardly obey and are just waiting for the chance to rebel. This theoretical supposition does not come from any scriptural descriptions of that Millennial kingdom (unless they invoke passages which are not about that age, but about the age following it, the post-Millennial age).

However, they then have to explain where so many wicked unbelievers came from in that Millennial Kingdom age. Many, if not most (including Richardson), argue that there will be many wicked unbelievers who will survive God's judgment at the second coming of Christ, to enter into that Millenial kingdom. This they maintain despite the fact that passage after passage tells us that all the unsaved will be destroyed, and in fact the whole earth will be completely destroyed, such as Zephaniah 1:2-18 and 3:8 and 2 Peter 3:8-13. Certainly there is nothing in this book of Revelation to suggest that God's judgment is anything less than universal, including the whole earth - men's arguments and manipulation of words notwithstanding. So the truth is that if we accept their explanations we actually have to accept the obvious implications that scripture contradicts itself if we take it literally - the same men who insist we need to take it literally to get their interpretations (huh?).

While men are quite capable of confusing scripture, it is not scripture that confuses men. The prophetic scripture is actually rather clear and pretty unambiguous if we let it speak for itself. There will be an Antichrist, the Beast of Daniel and Revelation. It or he will not be the Harlot Babylon, the religious element, which he in fact destroys. It will also not be Gog of Magog, which doesn't appear on the scene until over a thousand years after the Tribulation Period is over and Christ returns in judgment on the whole earth. Men who are looking for Gog and his armies to appear soon, are going to be disappointed, and those who believe them may become disillusioned with Bible prophecy. Whether the forces of Ezekiel's Gog are Russia and/or a coalition of Arabic/Persian nations, or not, is not particularly relevant at this time (which is not to say they are of no importance). However, it is quite believable that the same group of nations which are in rebellion against God during the Tribulation Period, will also resume their rebellion against God once they are brought back to earth along with their real leader,

Satan, after 1000 years of imprisonment during the Millennial reign of Christ on earth. It is not so believable that such a huge global conflict will not even be mentioned in the book of Revelation, or that the Antichrist is actually this Gog and John just failed to make that connection for us.

All of this is to discern between what we should not be looking for, to help identify accurately what we should be looking for. One of the reasons why Bible prophecy has become a matter of such ridicule and incredulity in our world today is because of all the wrong interpretations that men have derived from it. Too many have come up with and proclaimed loudly that Jesus would return in their life time, setting dates or timeframes which have of course already come and gone - no Jesus. How many times can we cry "wolf" and expect anybody to listen. Men have proclaimed that the Antichrist was Nero, Hitler or Mussolini (the Roman connection), or Gorbachev, or a president of the United States, to name but a few. In more recent times it was Russia or some say China, the Catholic Church, and now the European Union, which will make up the government of the Antichrist. Yet it seems now fairly clear that some of those were just very mistaken, and some touted today are appearing less and less feasible in light of world trends, developments and events.

Then we have the more palatable teachings that make it all pretty irrelevant to us, such as the Pre-tribulation Rapture theory, which is itself controversial. The net effect of that is that many if not most pastors and would-be Bible teachers prefer to avoid the subject of end-time prophecy altogether, saying that it doesn't really matter what we believe on this subject, we just need to live right. The fact that this is in essence writing off about a third of scripture as being unimportant and irrelevant doesn't seem to be a problem for them. The fact that we are given this information so that we can know what we need to know in order to live right during those last days, and to give us the motivation we need to live right in any age, escapes their awareness. The fact that there is controversy over what the Bible is telling us on these subjects is no more reason to ignore and avoid them than any other truths of God's word, all of which are under attack at one time or another, especially in this age in which we live. Jesus, Paul, John, Peter, James and Jude did not avoid controversial subjects to keep the peace and promote unity, nor should we.

The fact is that the world, and thus worldlings, do not want to hear most of the Biblical truths, one of which is the fact that this world is facing judgments and a catastrophic end. The message of Bible prophecy is pessimistic to those who do not want to submit to the sovereignty of God - and they hate it. But it seems that such is a message God wants them, and all of us, to hear. Our archenemy, Satan, wants to try any way he can to negate or at dilute, or at least distract us from what God is trying to communicate to us. He is accomplishing this today among professing believers by causing us to question the relevance and importance of such communications, thereby getting us to disregard and virtually ignore, or just reject, what God is trying to tell us. Of course he does so in the name of promoting such good things, as unity and peace between us. For some he is using the disillusionment with so many false interpretations and scenarios, which eventually prove to be in some cases almost comical if they weren't so tragic. Thus the seed of doubt is planted, growing into unhealthy skepticism, such that people become so turned off on the subject matter that they also choose to ignore or avoid it. Congratulations Satan - you are accomplishing your objectives.

The answer to so many false interpretations and scenarios is not to reject them all and avoid the whole subject, but to learn how to accurately discern what the Bible is saying and what it is not saying - "*accurately handling the word of truth*" (2 Timothy 2:15). There are not many accurate interpretations of what God is trying to communicate. He is not a God of ambivalence and ambiguity, but He has clear thoughts about everything, and He inspired men to write them in human languages, in ways that are neither ambivalent nor ambiguous. But as with any communications written or otherwise, there are objective rules of interpretation that must be followed. Communications involving rational thought processes require the interpreter to follow rules of rational thinking, which we usually call logic, to derive a rational and accurate meaning. In the case of scripture we have what is called the disciplines of Hermeneutics, and Exegesis, which involve rules that must be followed to accurately interpret what the authors of scripture wrote, and what they meant. Then of course when we have different languages involved, the correct exegesis requires one to know and apply the rules associated with the grammar, and syntax, of the various languages involved, as well as the accurate translation of the specific words used. In the case of the Bible we have Hebrew, Aramaic, and Greek, which have to be accurately translated. All of these play key roles in getting to the intended message God was trying to communicate.

Without exception, wrong interpretations of Bible prophecy which have come and gone, and some which are still popular or becoming popular today, violate some or all of these rules associated with Hermeneutics, Logic, or Exegesis and Translation. In most cases, words found in scripture are changed or modified or just replaced with other words, or meanings are forced upon them that do not come from the text. Often words or phrases are taken out of context. More often than not the interpreter engages in circular reasoning to make their case. In probably all cases they approach the subject, and in turn the words or the passages, with presuppositions and preconceptions about what they think they should say, and they then attempt to make it say something that that is compatible with their view on the subject. It is sometimes amazing how accomplished men become at such an art, with the result that they can be very convincing to others, who don't critically examine what they are doing and saying.

While it is the conscious attempt of this student of scripture to avoid these pitfalls, by first becoming very aware of such presuppositions and preconceptions, and then to know and follow those rules of hermeneutics, logic, exegesis and translation, no one is infallible. However, the interpretations and conclusions and proposals presented herein should be critically evaluated based on those very same rules and principles. Admittedly it is unlikely that everything being presented as the correct interpretation will be 100% correct, or that the scenarios described will all happen exactly as I have portrayed them. But hopefully it will cause some to think, and to look critically at what is going on in the world, and to reconsider what the Bible is saying about the future, and how it applies and relates to the developments in our world today.

Chapter 4 Summary and Conclusions - What's the Point?

The point is, we are living in a mad world (what's new?) in which there are forces in play which seem to be very out of control, and increasingly so as the days go by. Men don't seem to have answers that make any sense, for the rapid spread of violence and terror around the globe, threatening virtually every community on the face of this earth. Facing the prospect of religious extremists, who are already terrorizing the rest of the world, becoming nuclear powers, is a matter of grave concern (to make the understatement of the year), or certainly should be for everyone on the planet. Given that diplomatic solutions involve making treaties and agreements with an avowed enemy whose religion tells them it is righteous for them to lie and deceive and make deals that they have no intention of keeping, it is a fool's errand.   But given that military solutions are also deemed unacceptable, and indeed have little prospects of an acceptable outcome, what possible answers are there? Men don't have the answers.

The point is that we don't really have to rely on men, whose track record is at best not one that inspires confidence, but we do have a reliable source to which we can turn. The fact is that the Bible has a well-documented track record of being very accurate and reliable at predicting what will happen on the grand scale of global trends and events - ignorant people just don't know about it. Despite the broad-based ignorance of men down through the ages, in fact God has revealed in amazing detail what would happen since the beginning of civilization in the cradle of civilization, the Sumer and Akkadian cultures, which became Babylon. We show in the preceding discussions that Daniel predicted the Babylonian Empire's rise and fall, and the rise and fall of the succeeding Medo-Persian and Alexandrian Empires, and the succession of the Seleucid line of kings down to Antiochus IV Epiphanes of the second century BC. We see that Daniel's predictions involved incredible amounts of detail, which defies explanation apart from the supernatural divine revelation. We make the rather obvious point that with that kind of track record, only a fool would ignore what the Bible predicts about the future, which it turns out is very connected with the past.

The point is that we have very meaningful and relevant predictions, some of which are actually finding fulfillment in our world today. From the predicted re-emergence of Israel as a nation in recent history, to the rise of Islam and the Mid-Eastern Mesopotamian region to become the center of attention on the world's stage, the incredible correlation to the predictions of Daniel and John is impressive if not amazing. If this is not enough to get our attention, we must be either willfully blind, or just somewhat brain dead.

The point is that we have some pretty clear predictions, including dire warnings, about what is going to happen, with details that will leave little doubt for the informed rational thinking person about where it is all headed. For the believer who responds appropriately to the message there will be little need for panic, or overwhelming distress, in spite of the otherwise terrifying developments and events that are going to be happening. To the unbeliever, or the uninformed or misinformed believer, the natural response will be everything from confusion to desperation and probably terror, with many abandoning their former faith, succumbing to the deception, enticements, or threats of the system of the Antichrist. Those who are now so sure they won't even be here when the Antichrist begins to impose his reign of terror, * may not be able to recognize him for who he is. They may take his mark, the *"mark of the beast,"* not knowing what it is (it probably won't be a visible tattoo with three sixes), in order to survive. They may be among those Paul wrote about in 2 Thessalonians:

> *"[8]Then that lawless one will be revealed whom the Lord will slay with the breath of His mouth and bring to an end by the appearance of His coming; [9]that is, the one whose coming is*

in accord with the activity of Satan, with all power and signs and false wonders, [10]and with all the deception of wickedness for those who perish, because they did not receive the love of the truth so as to be saved. [11]For this reason God will send upon them a deluding influence so that they will believe what is false, [12]in order that they all may be judged who did not believe the truth, but took pleasure in wickedness." (2 Thessalonians 2:8-12)

*[One of the problems with the Pretribulation Rapture view - those who really believe it will think it can't be the Antichrist because they believe they will be raptured out before he can appear. This combined with the false belief in a "once-saved-always-saved" doctrine, will make them think that they can take the mark of the beast, which they probably won't even recognize, and not lose their salvation. Such a combination of erroneous teachings could be the recipe for the eternal disaster incurred by those who *"did not receive the love of the truth"* and thus *"did not believe the truth"* (2 Thessalonians 2:9-12).]

The point is that people need to be paying attention to what the God of the universe has said. They, or we, need to know what actually is predicted, and be able to recognize what is not - false interpretations and teachings that are in error - to be able to recognize what is. They, or we, need to cultivate a love for God's truth, and find out what it is, and embrace it - to do otherwise is to play the fool. Then, we need to act accordingly, with rational responses to what God has said.

That of course begins with accepting the reality that only God has the answer to man's problems. The first most basic answer is in the provision of His son, Jesus Christ, as the only solution to the most basic problem - that we all fall short of God's standard of acceptable righteousness (i.e. the sin problem - Romans 3:23). Believing and accepting what God says He has provided as the solution to our problem, that is accepting Jesus Christ as the only savior from our lost condition and our hopeless situation, is the next critical step (Romans 6:23, John 1:12, 3:16, 5:24, 14:6, and Romans 10:9-10). Becoming born of the spirit of God (John 3:3-9), receiving His spiritual life, which is the eternal life (John 3:16, 4:14), which is also the "abundant life" (John10:10) is essential to escaping the condition of spiritual death, into which we are born physically

(Romans 5:12, Ephesians 2:1-5). Having received this life of the Spirit of God in us we need to continue in that walk of faith, as followers of Christ - what the Bible calls walking in the Spirit (Galatians 5:16-25), becoming spiritually minded (Romans 8:1-14), having our minds reprogrammed by God's truth so that our lives become transformed (Romans 12:1-2). This is what the Bible calls "the Gospel."

However, we are also instructed that it is the truth that sets us free (John 8:32) through the Word of God (John 6:63, Hebrews 4:12, 2 Timothy 3:16, 1 Peter 2:2) and the enlightenment of the Spirit of God (John 14:26, 1 John 2:27). These are realities we could not know anything about, if it were not revealed to us by a supreme being we call God. No matter what we know or don't know about prophecy, or what the future holds, it isn't very important until we know about and deal appropriately with these fundamental realities. The one question everyone will have to answer is who is Jesus - and we better get it right. If our answer is that He was a good man, or a great teacher, or even a great prophet, we are right, but we got the wrong answer. If that is all we think He is we are calling Him a lunatic, or a liar (1 John 5:10) - since He claimed to be God (John 10:30), the only way for men to be saved (John 14:6, 3:18, 8:24).

With respect to the main focus of this book, we can consider the evidence which is so unequivocally clear in light of the Bible's record for reliability with respect to its record at predicting the most significant events throughout history with incredible accuracy. Or we can ignore it, or choose to be ignorant of it, to our own peril. Similarly, we can pay attention to what it is telling us about what is going on in our world, and why, and what is going to happen in the future, or we can ignore it, or choose not to believe it, that is left up to us. But knowing what we can and should know, such as what is discussed in the preceding pages, who would want to bet their life's savings on the Bible's predictions being wrong this time - let alone their life, and their eternal destiny?

Sources

Brooks, Rodney, <u>Fields of Color: The Theory that Escaped Einstein</u>.

Cornuke, Robert, <u>Temple - Amazing New Discoveries That Change Everything About the Location of Solomon's Temple</u>.

Davidson, Mark, <u>Daniel Revisited.</u>

Durant, Will, <u>The Story of Civilization, The Age of Faith</u>.

<u>Funk and Wagnall's New Encyclopedia</u> 1983.

Green, Jay P., <u>The Interlinear Hebrew-Aramaic Old Testament</u>, Vol. III of <u>The Interlinear Hebrew-Greek-English Bible</u>, 2nd ed., 1985.

Hawking, Stephen, <u>A Brief History of Time</u>.

Hislop, Rev. Alexander, <u>The Two Babylons - or The Papal Worship.</u>

Richardson, Joel, <u>Mideast Beast: The Scriptural Case for an Islamic Antichrist.</u>

Silva, Rodrigo, <u>The Coming Bible Prophecy Reformation</u>.

Simons, Geoff, <u>Iraq, From Sumer to Saddam</u>, 2nd edition, 1996.

Sookhdeo, Patrick, <u>Global Jihad - The Future in the Face of Militant Islam.</u>

Spencer, Robert, <u>Stealth Jihad</u>, 2008.

Thomas, Robert L., ed., <u>New American Standard Exhaustive Concordance of the Bible, Hebrew-Aramaic and Greek Dictionaries</u>, 1981.

Tregelles, Samuel Prideaux , LL. D., <u>Gesenius' Hebrew and Chaldee Lexicon to the Old Testament Scriptures</u>, 1979.